origami QUILTS

TOMOKO FUSE

JAPAN PUBLICATIONS TRADING COMPANY

©2001 by Tomoko Fuse
All rights reserved, including the right to reproduce this book or portions
thereof in any form without the written permission of the publisher.
Translated by Kazuhiko Nagai
Photographs by Sasuke Hamakawa
Published by Japan Publications Trading Co., Ltd.,
1-2-1 Sarugaku-cho, Chiyoda-ku, Tokyo, 101-0064 Japan.

First printing: May 2001

Japanese language edition published by Chikuma Shobo Publishing Co., Ltd.,
Tokyo in 1995 titled "ORIGAMI KIRUTO." Copyright © Tomoko Fuse

Distributors:
United States: Kodansha America, Inc. through Oxford University Press,
198 Madison Avenue, New York, NY 10016.
Canada: Fitzhenry & Whiteside Ltd.,
195 Allstate Parkway, Markham, Ontario L3R 4T8.
United Kingdom and Europe: Premier Book Marketing Ltd.,
Clarendon House, 52, Cornmarket Street, Oxford OX1 3HJ, England.
Australia and New Zealand: Bookwise International Pty Ltd.,
174 Cormack Road, Wingfield, South Australia 5013, Australia.
Asia and Japan: Japan Publications Trading Co., Ltd.,
1-2-1 Sarugaku-cho, Chiyoda-ku, Tokyo, 101-0064 Japan.

ISBN 4-88996-068-6

Printed in Japan

Contents

Preface

One day I happened to get to work on a plain unit origami. It was so delightful that I was absorbed in it. I enjoyed various patterns by assembling square, triangle and pentagon units and trying to lock different pieces of paper. So far the unit origami has been three-dimensional, but the plain unit origami is different. It is a free and flowery world. It has brought me new pleasure.

When you stop to think about it, unit origami is a combination of parts, so it is natural that it leads up to the patchwork quilt. You can make use of remnants of scraps of paper to make a quilt. It depends on your idea. A variety of methods are applicable from a simple design to an elaborate one. Just start from the design, which suits your fancy.

If you try two or three works, you will certainly find that 'origami quilt' is different from those, which use scissors or glue.

The combination of units is interesting itself, but the color and pattern of paper play an important role in the excellent result. This is one of the fascinating points of 'origami quilt' like that of cloth quilt. The practical use of paper quilt in our daily life is limited, but it is delightful to make it, since it has an element of puzzle and it displays unique patterns only origami can produce. It is up to you to design a splendid 'origami quilt,' using various colorful paper.

March 28, 2001
Tomoko Fuse

List of Color Illustrations

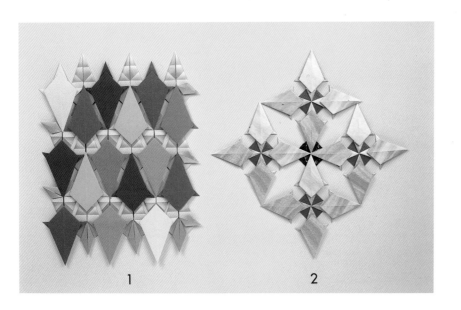

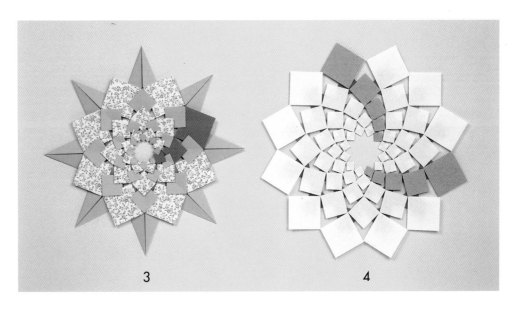

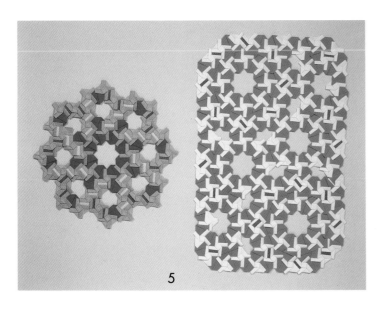

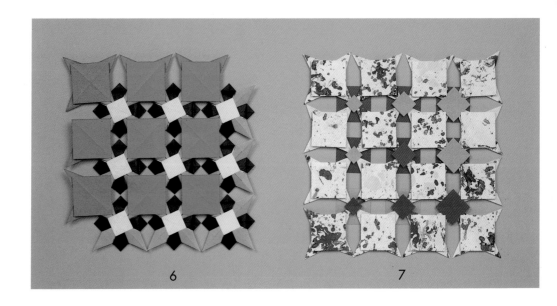

6   7

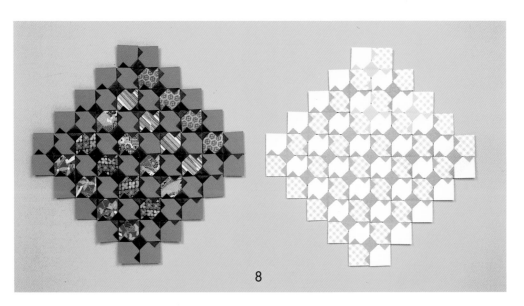

8

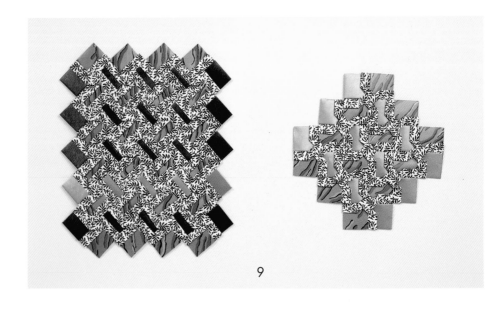

9

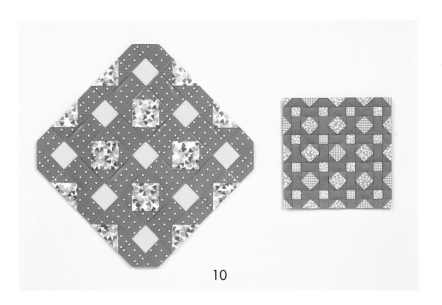

10

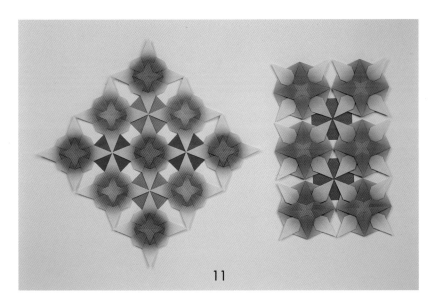

11

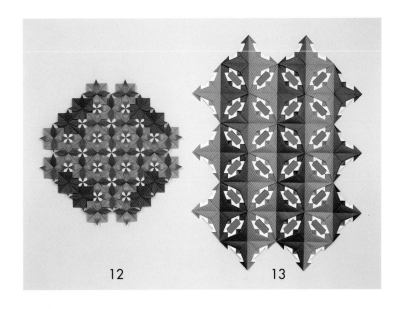

12   13

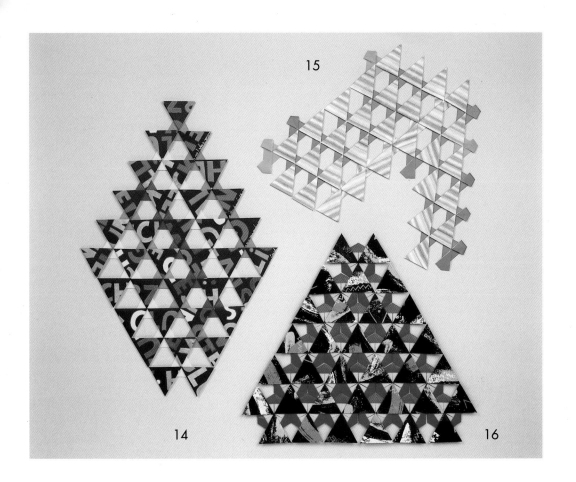

15

14

16

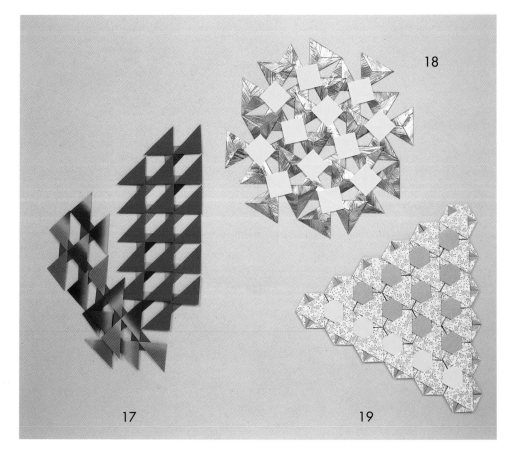

18

17

19

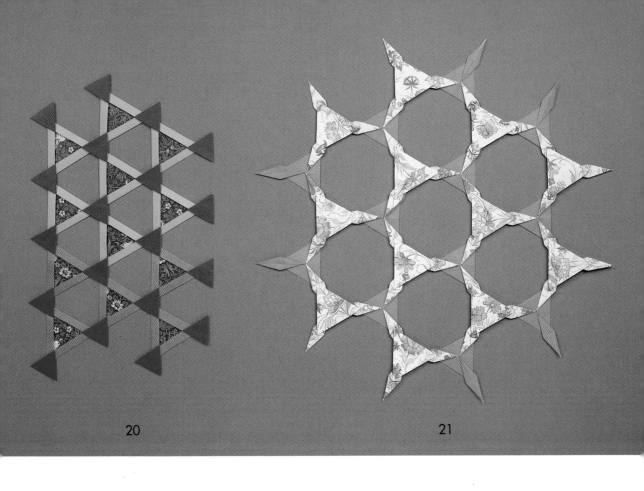

20

21

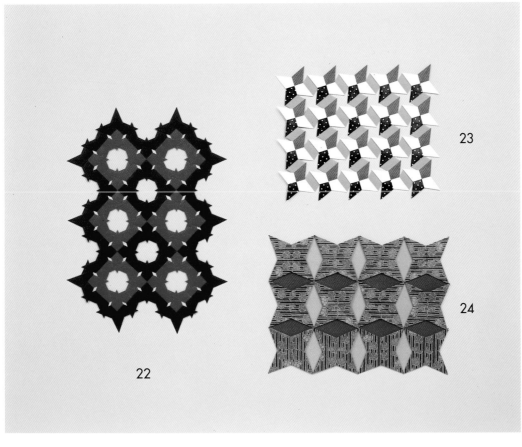

22

23

24

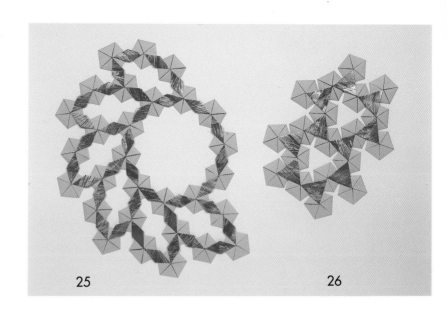

25

26

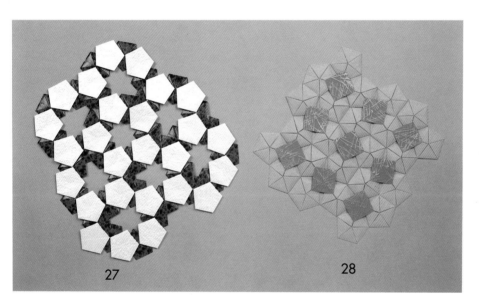

27

28

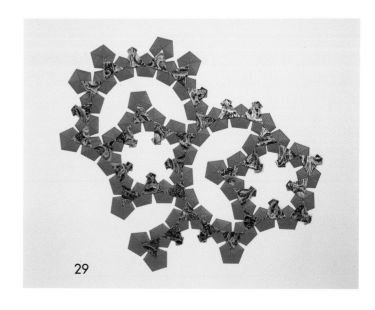

29

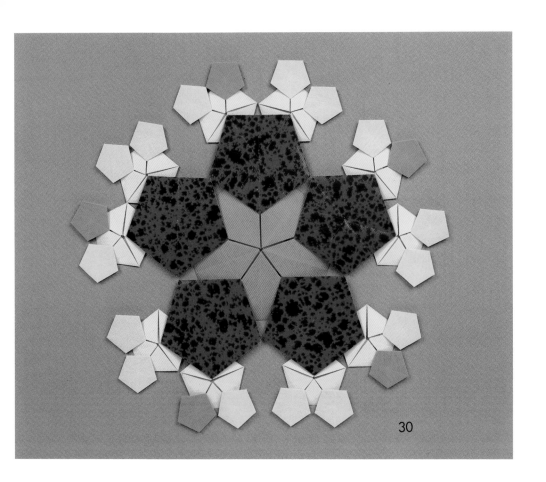

30

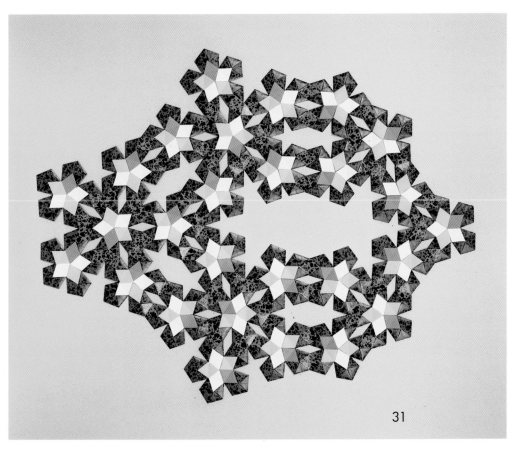

31

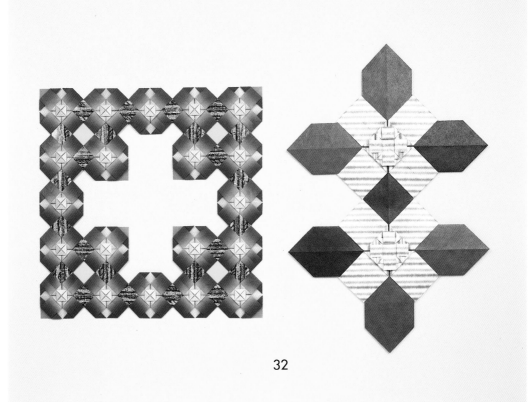

32

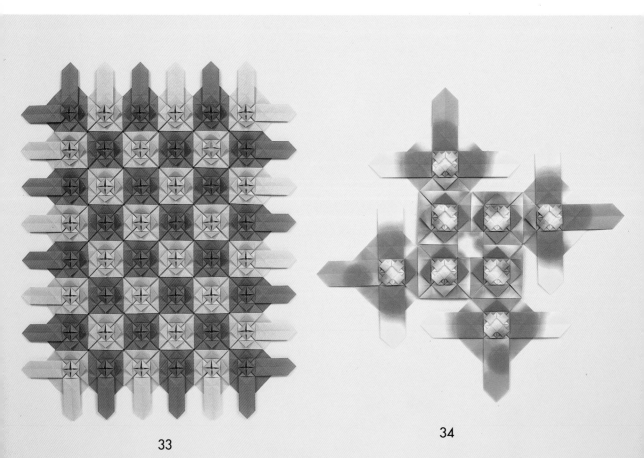

33

34

Symbols and Folding Techniques

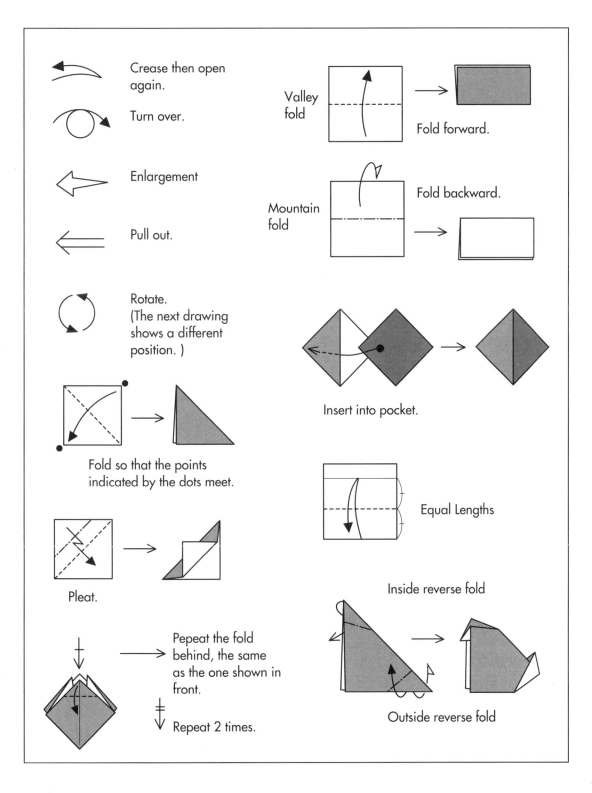

Crease then open again.

Turn over.

Enlargement

Pull out.

Rotate. (The next drawing shows a different position.)

Fold so that the points indicated by the dots meet.

Pleat.

Pepeat the fold behind, the same as the one shown in front.

Repeat 2 times.

Valley fold

Fold forward.

Mountain fold

Fold backward.

Insert into pocket.

Equal Lengths

Inside reverse fold

Outside reverse fold

Crosses

You may join these cross units with horns each other or lock with different units. They are very valuable units.

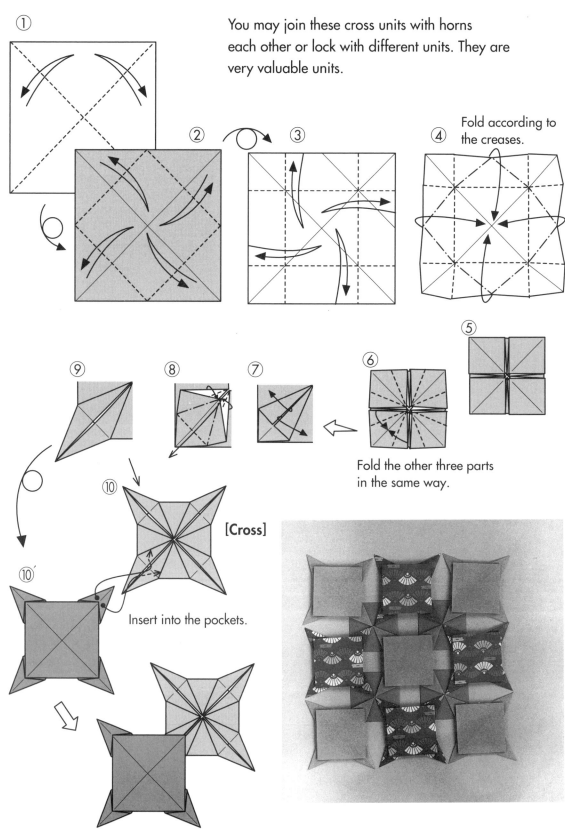

④ Fold according to the creases.

⑥ Fold the other three parts in the same way.

[Cross]

Insert into the pockets.

Crosses + Squares

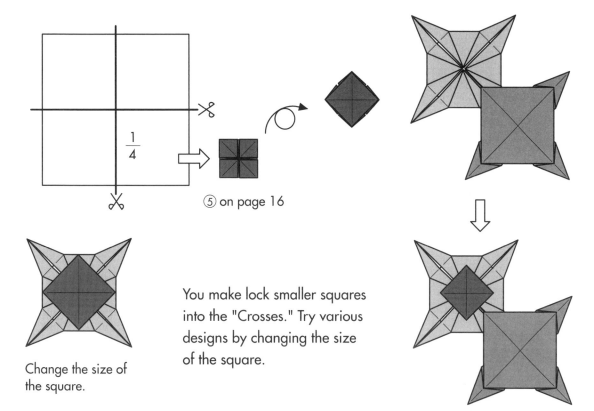

$\frac{1}{4}$

⑤ on page 16

You make lock smaller squares into the "Crosses." Try various designs by changing the size of the square.

Change the size of the square.

Double Crosses + Crosses

To make this unit, place two crosses one upon another and fix on top with a small, ¼ cross. You may employ various locking methods. Both sides, back and front, look very interesting.

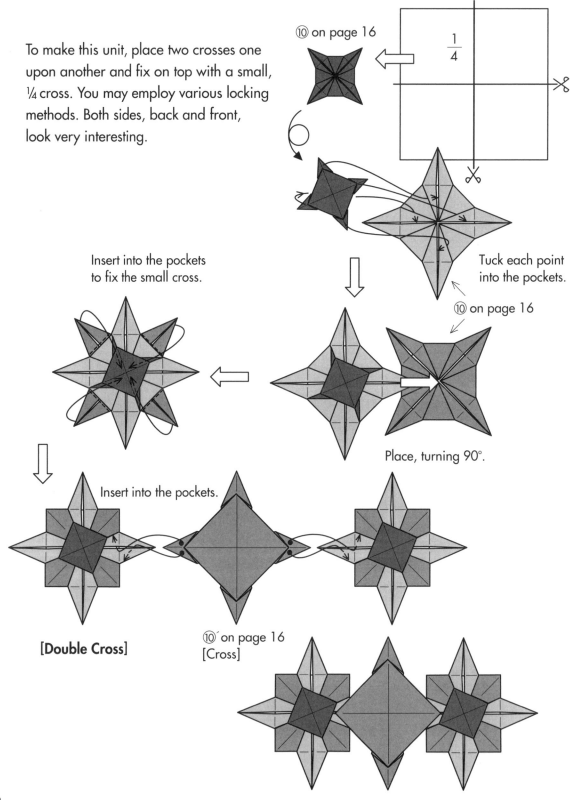

⑩ on page 16

$\frac{1}{4}$

Tuck each point into the pockets.

⑩ on page 16

Insert into the pockets to fix the small cross.

Place, turning 90°.

Insert into the pockets.

[Double Cross]

⑩´ on page 16
[Cross]

Front

Back

As shown on page 17, you may fix "square" and assemble in the same way.

Double Crosses + Joints

First assemble "Double Crosses" and then
combine the square joint on the corner.
You can obtain a thick finish. It is possible
to mix with other units or change sizes,
and you can enjoy variations.

► Jointing Unit ◄

[Double Cross] on page 18

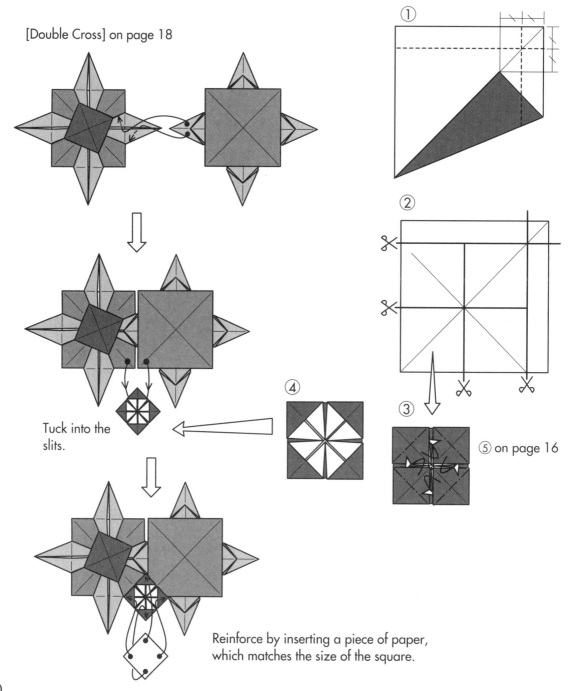

Tuck into the
slits.

⑤ on page 16

Reinforce by inserting a piece of paper,
which matches the size of the square.

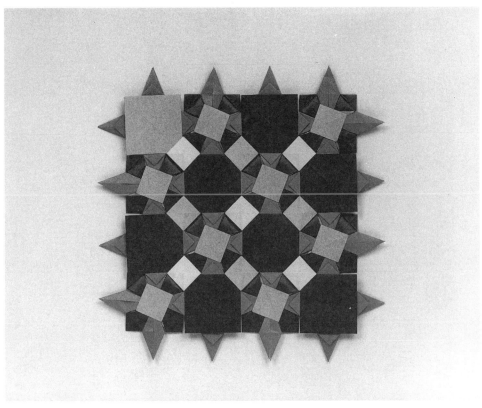

Crosses + Joints

Make gradually smaller units; a cross unit the size of ¼ of the original and then the one the size of ¼ of the scale-down unit. Assemble the units by joints.

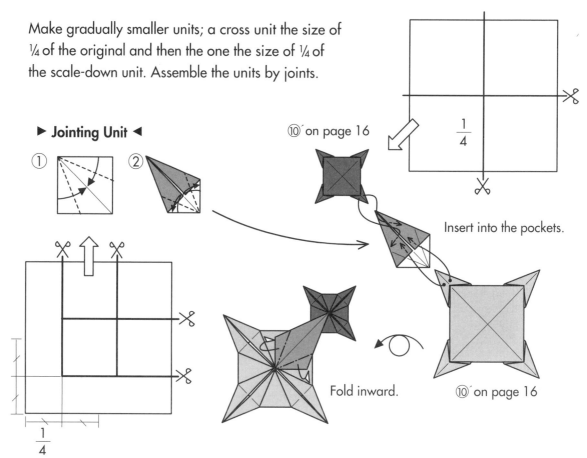

▶ **Jointing Unit** ◀

① ②

⑩´ on page 16

$\frac{1}{4}$

Insert into the pockets.

$\frac{1}{4}$

Fold inward.

⑩´ on page 16

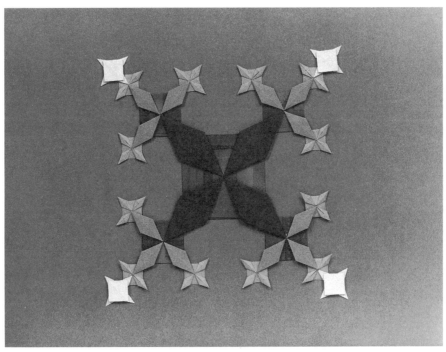

Square Windows

Square windows come out one after another when units are joined one by one. You may make a patchwork by inserting waste pieces of paper or scraps of colored paper into the windows.

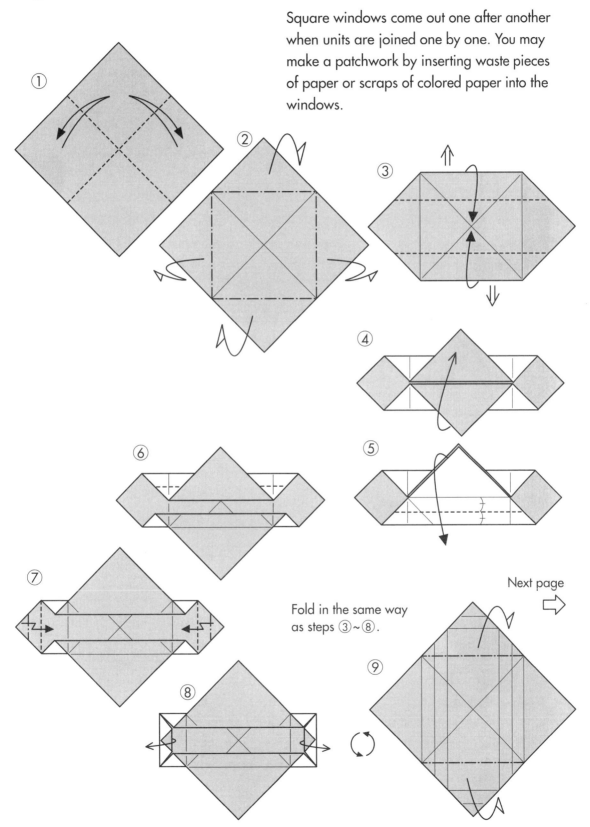

Fold in the same way as steps ③~⑧.

Next page ⇨

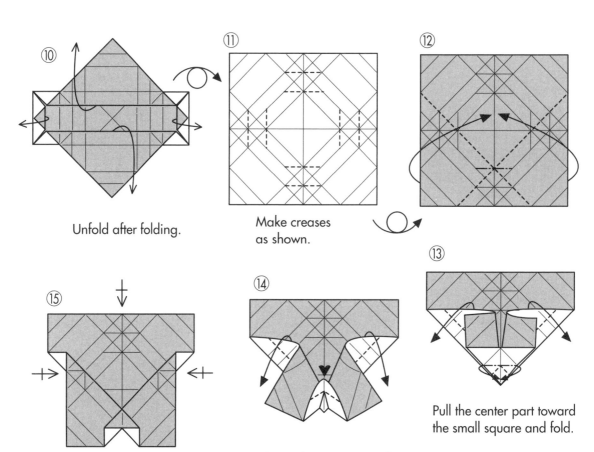

⑩ Unfold after folding.

⑪ Make creases as shown.

⑫

⑬ Pull the center part toward the small square and fold.

⑭ Open the center triangle and squash. Open wide to left and right.

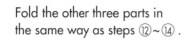

⑮ Fold the other three parts in the same way as steps ⑫ ~ ⑭ .

⑯ Fold backward.

Insert into the slit.

Insert into the under pocket.

Insert other pieces of paper or photos into the square windows, (a) and (b).

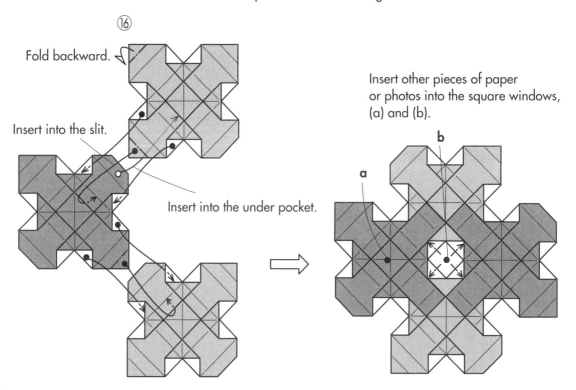

a

b

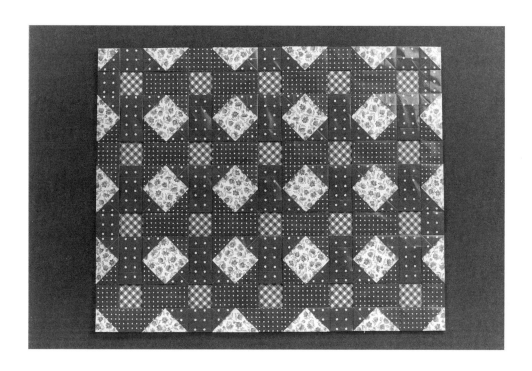

The illustration shows the size of paper to be inserted.
Paper with colorful patterns, photos or illustrations
will be good for your free arrangement.

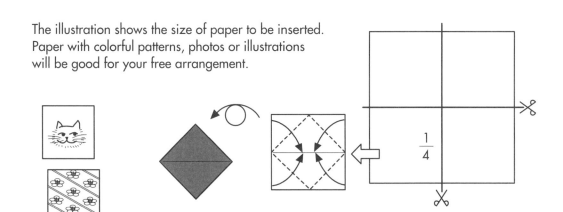

Four-Petaled Flowers + Crosses

Make flowers with four petals and join them with crosses.

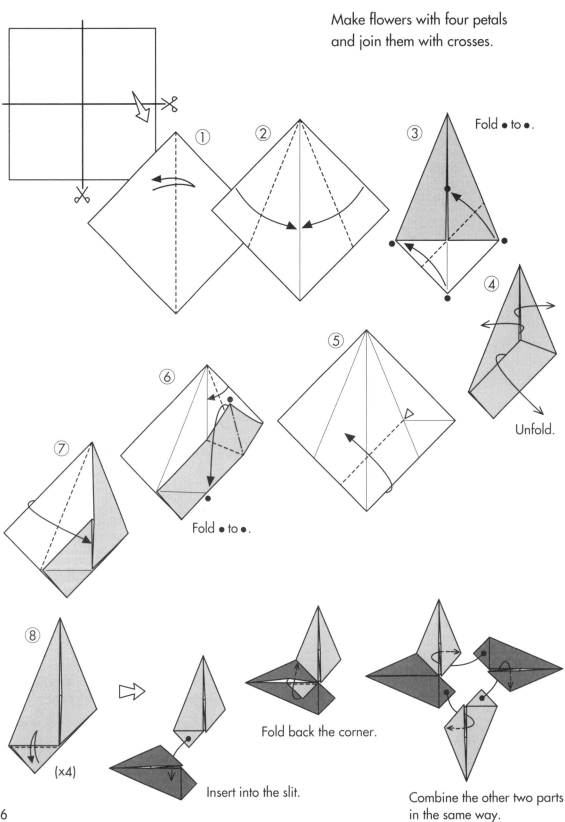

① ② ③ Fold ● to ●.

④ Unfold.

⑤ ⑥ Fold ● to ●.

⑦

⑧ (×4)

Insert into the slit.

Fold back the corner.

Combine the other two parts in the same way.

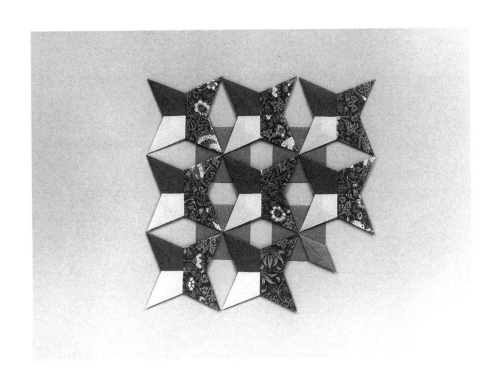

⑩´ [Cross] on page 16

Insert into the pockets.

Combine the units
in this way.

[Front]

[Back]

[Front]

[Four-Petaled Flower]

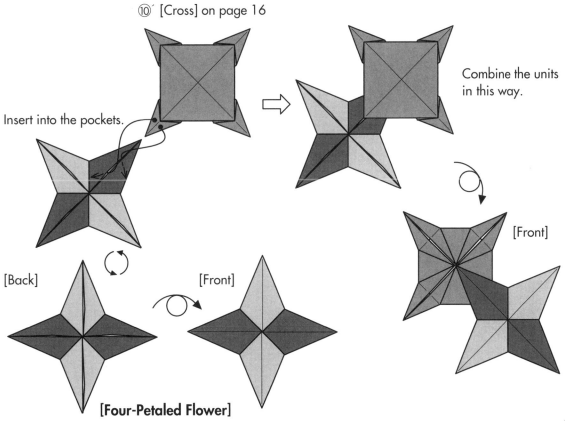

Four-Petaled Flowers + Half-Crosses

▶ **Half-Cross 1** ◀

Half-Cross unit 1 can be joined in two ways, A and B. You may change the size of Four-Petaled units or try other combinations.

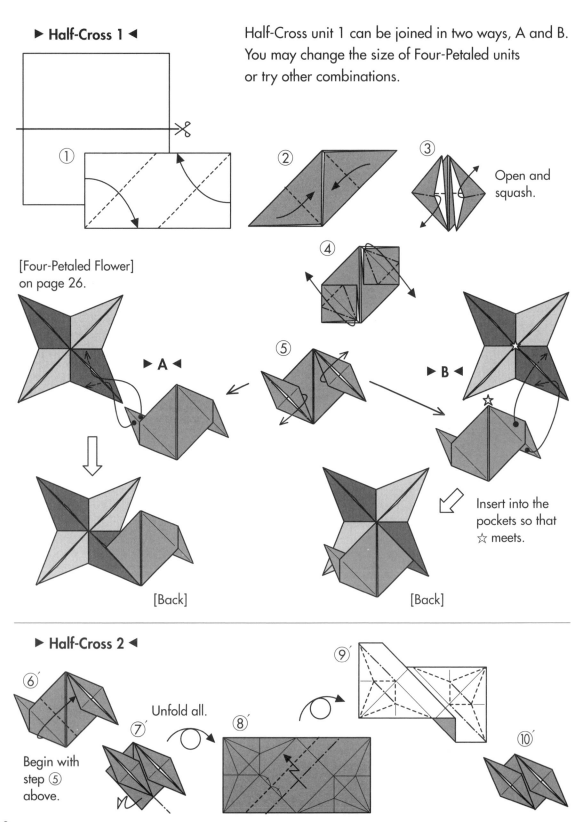

[Four-Petaled Flower] on page 26.

▶ **A** ◀

⑤

▶ **B** ◀

Open and squash.

Insert into the pockets so that ☆ meets.

[Back]

[Back]

▶ **Half-Cross 2** ◀

⑥′

Begin with step ⑤ above.

⑦′

Unfold all.

⑧′

⑨′

⑩′

Four-Petaled Flowers + Half-Crosses 1–A

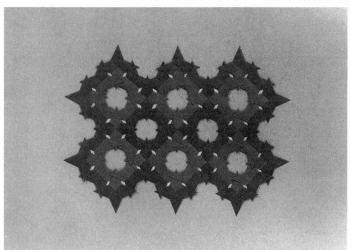

Four-Petaled Flowers + Half-Crosses 1–B

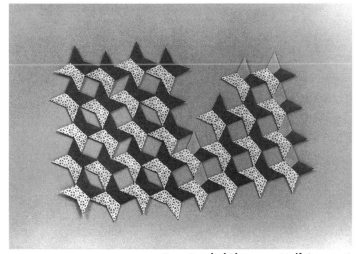

Four-Petaled Flowers + Half-Crosses 2

Flower Crosses + Crosses & Others

by Mihoko Kittaka

The more opening slits you have, the more you may enjoy various methods of joining. This unit suits the purpose. How the article turns out is up to your sense.

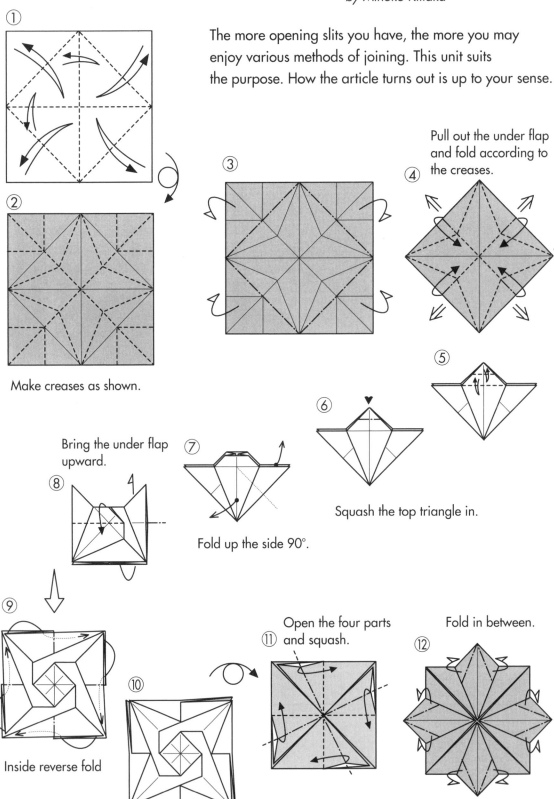

①

② Make creases as shown.

③

④ Pull out the under flap and fold according to the creases.

⑤

⑥ Squash the top triangle in.

⑦ Fold up the side 90°.

⑧ Bring the under flap upward.

⑨ Inside reverse fold

⑩

⑪ Open the four parts and squash.

⑫ Fold in between.

You may cut paper in either way, A or B. Both become the same size.

▶ A ◀

[Back]

⑭

⑩ [Cross] on page 16.

See page 27 for the assembly.

⑬

▶ B ◀

[Front]

Variation of [Cross]

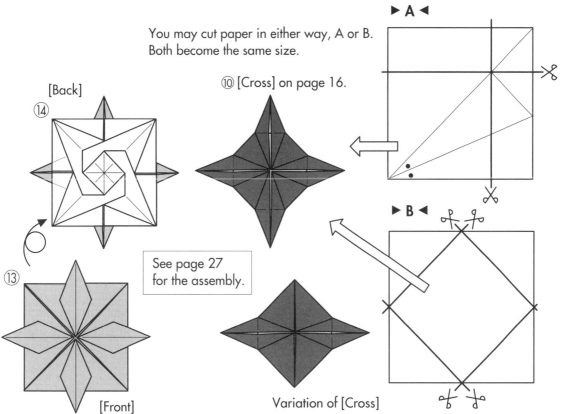

How to make
an Equilateral Triangle, Pentagon & Hexagon

Introduced here are how to fold triangles, pentagons and hexagons,
which are applicable to many cases. The fold of pentagon is more accurate
than the traditional one and it was worked out by Kunihiko Kasahara.

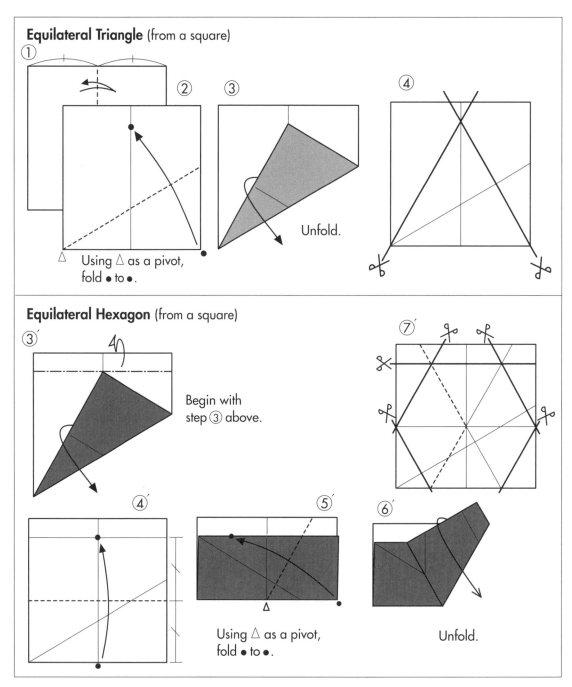

Equilateral Triangle (from a square)

①

②

③

④

Using △ as a pivot,
fold ● to ●.

Unfold.

Equilateral Hexagon (from a square)

③′

④′

Begin with
step ③ above.

⑦′

⑤′

Using △ as a pivot,
fold ● to ●.

⑥′

Unfold.

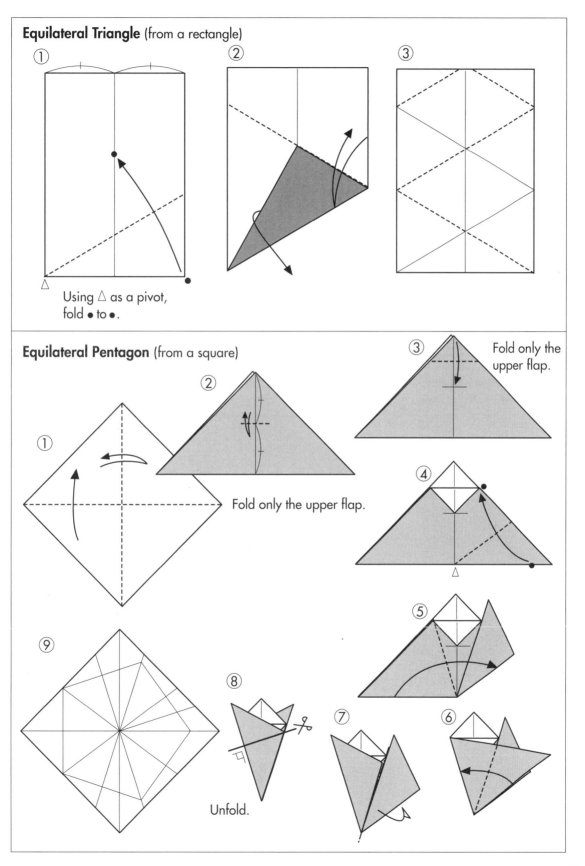

Equilateral Triangle (from a rectangle)

① Using △ as a pivot, fold ● to ●.

②

③

Equilateral Pentagon (from a square)

①

② Fold only the upper flap.

③ Fold only the upper flap.

④

⑤

⑥

⑦

⑧ Unfold.

⑨

33

Trefoils

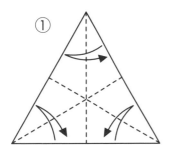

① Make creases as shown.

"Trefoils" of equilateral triangles form a counterpart to "Crosses" of squares. This triangle unit is also widely applicable. It is possible to join only the units of (B) below.

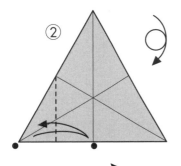

②

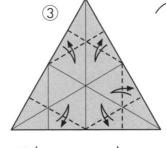

③ Make creases as shown.

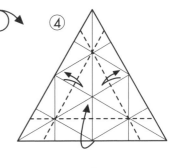

④

①´

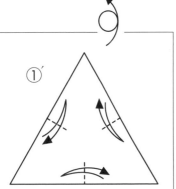

If you fold a bit as shown, unnecessary lines will not come out when completed.

⑤

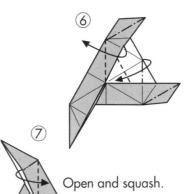

⑥

⑦ Open and squash.

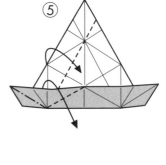

► A ◄   ⑧

[Trefoil]

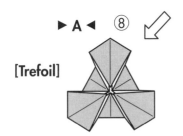

⑧´

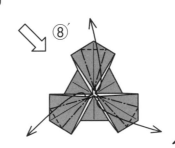

► B ◄

⑨´

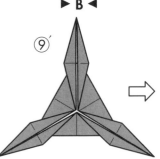

34

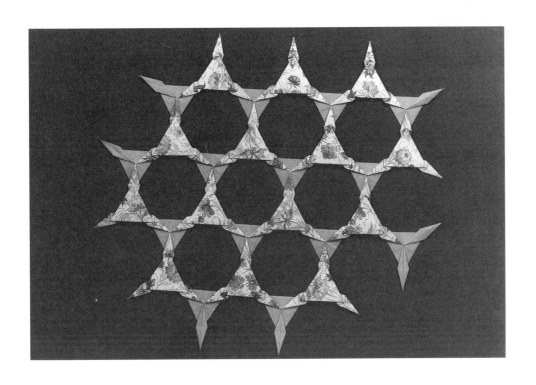

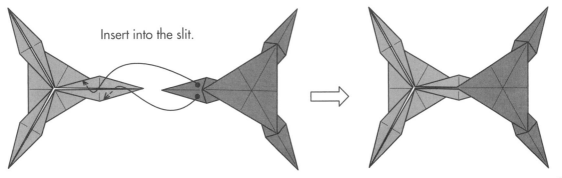

Insert into the slit.

Triangles with Slits

This triangle unit has slits on the surface.
If three cuts are made in step ④ , the finish will be neat.
If you don't like to make cuts, fold as directed in the box below.

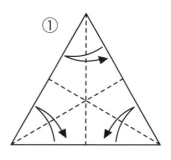

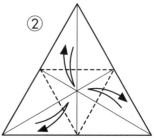

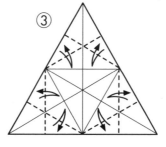

Make creases as shown.

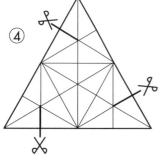

Make cuts.

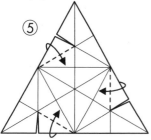

[Triangle with Slits]

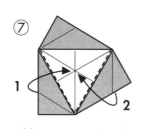

Fold in numerical order.

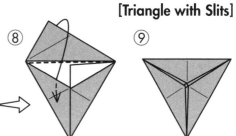

Fold into the pocket.

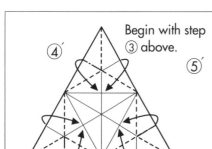

Begin with step ③ above.

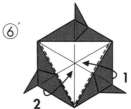

Fold in numerical order.

Fold into the pocket.

36

Trefoils + Triangles with Slits

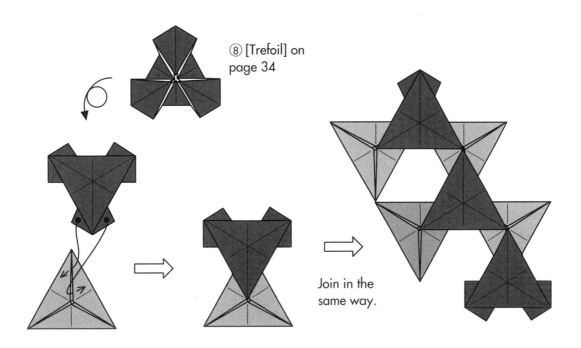

⑧ [Trefoil] on page 34

Join in the same way.

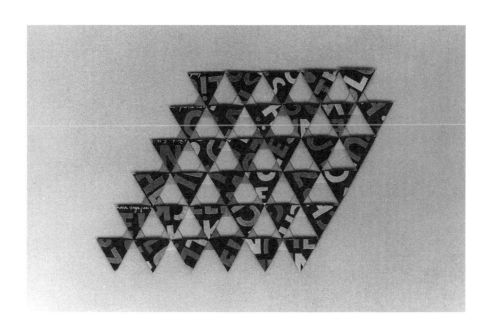

Triangles with Slits + Crosses

Make "Cross" units, which have the equal length of (a) of the "Triangle with Slits," and join them. Sides, back and front, look interesting.

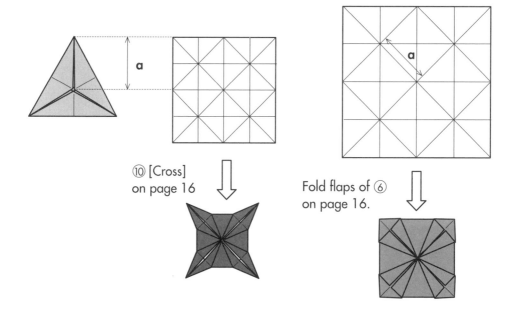

⑩ [Cross] on page 16

Fold flaps of ⑥ on page 16.

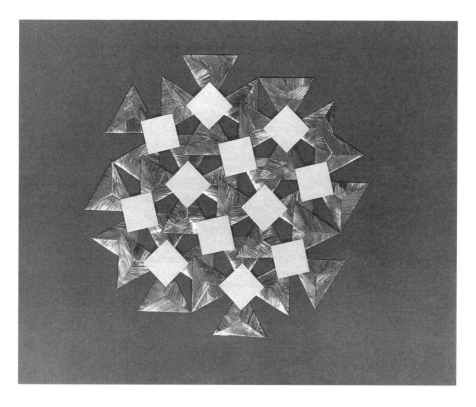

Triangles with Slits + Trefoil Variations

Fold the "Trefoil" so that it leaves a larger opening in the center and join the "Triangle with Slits" folded to match the size.

A variation of ⑧ [Trefoil] on page 34.

⑨ [Triangle with Slits] on page 36.

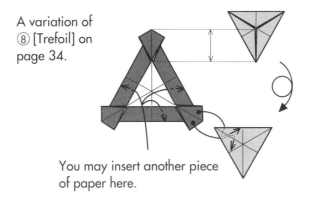

You may insert another piece of paper here.

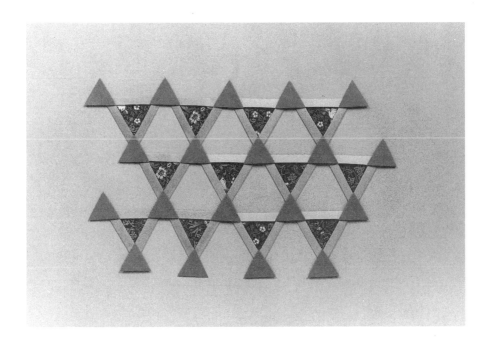

Hexagons with Outside Pleats
+ Triangles with Slits

Make hexagon units, which have pleats on the surface and insert the pleats into the slits of the "Triangles with Slits." In making the "Triangles with Slits," you may use lager paper than shown below.

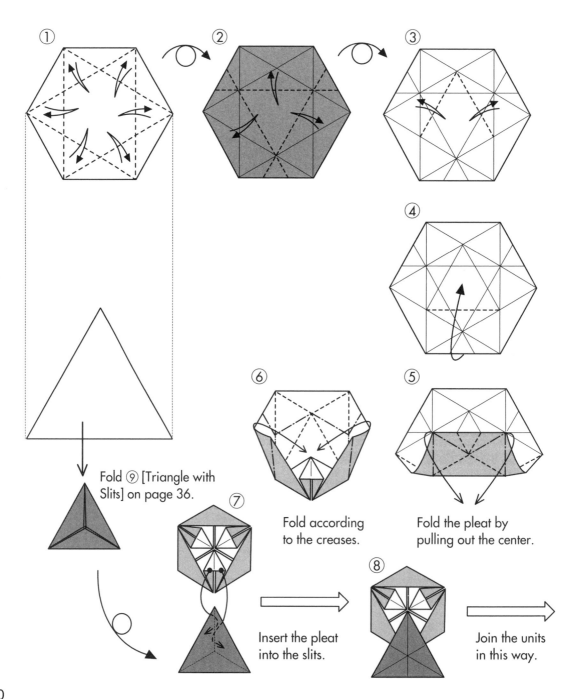

Fold ⑨ [Triangle with Slits] on page 36.

Fold according to the creases.

Fold the pleat by pulling out the center.

Insert the pleat into the slits.

Join the units in this way.

40

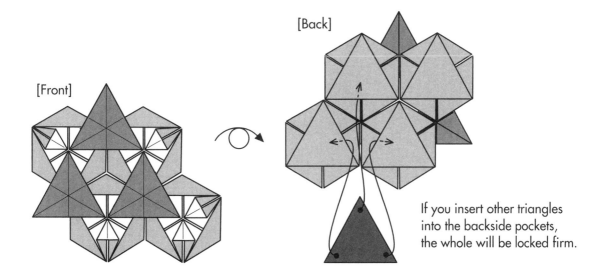

[Front]

[Back]

If you insert other triangles
into the backside pockets,
the whole will be locked firm.

Hexagons with Inside Pleats
+ Triangles with Slits

Fold so that the pleat is made between the inside and outside.
The following process is the same as given on the previous page.

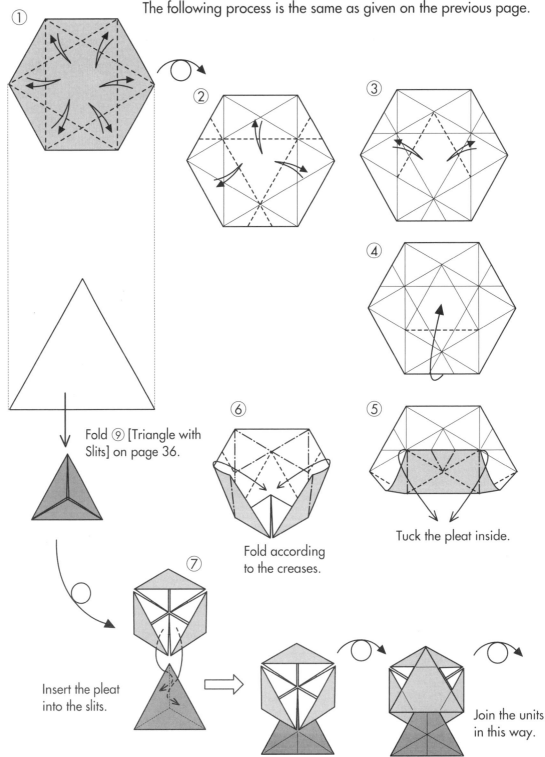

① ② ③

④

Fold ⑨ [Triangle with
Slits] on page 36.

⑥ ⑤

Fold according
to the creases.

Tuck the pleat inside.

⑦

Insert the pleat
into the slits.

Join the units
in this way.

Front

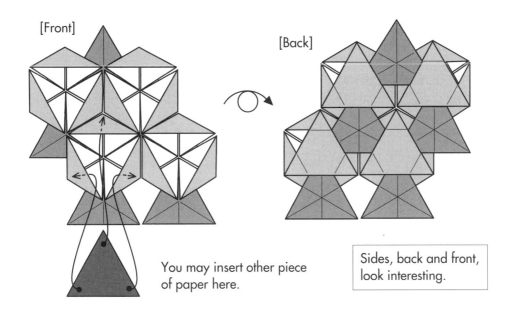

[Front]

[Back]

You may insert other piece of paper here.

Sides, back and front, look interesting.

43

Joining Triangles 1

Make a triangle by cutting square paper at a diagonal line, fold in the same way as steps on page 34 and join.
Try the unit with horns as in the box on the next page.

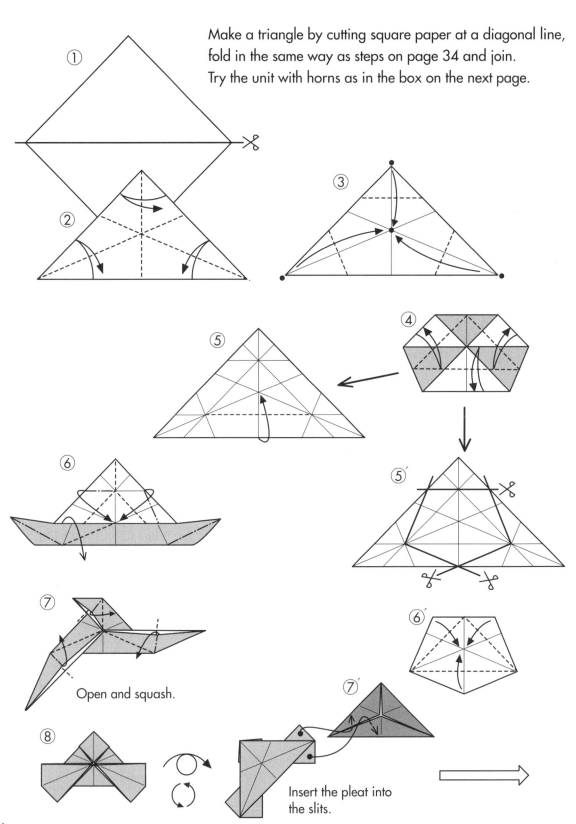

① ② ③ ④ ⑤ ⑤′ ⑥ ⑥′ ⑦ ⑦′ ⑧

Open and squash.

Insert the pleat into the slits.

Begin with step ⑧ on the left page.

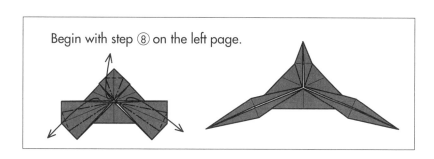

Join in either way, (a) or (b).

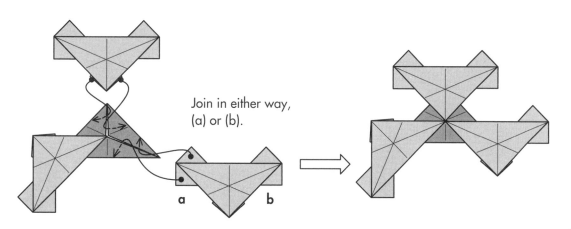

45

Joining Triangles 2

Join isosceles triangle units in the same way as steps on previous pages.
As long as shapes are the same, any triangle can be joined in this method.

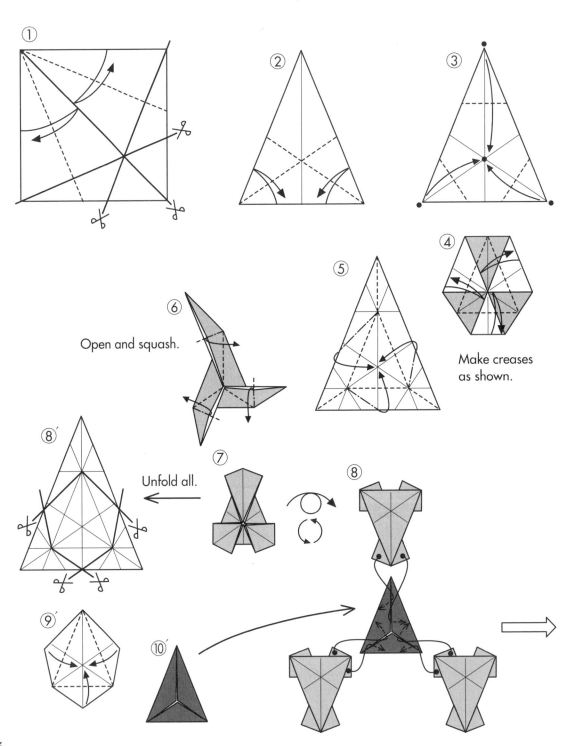

Open and squash.

Make creases as shown.

Unfold all.

Join units in this way.

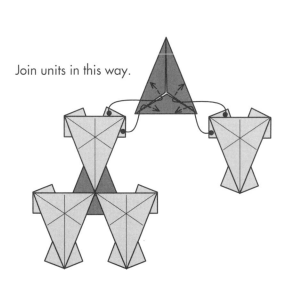

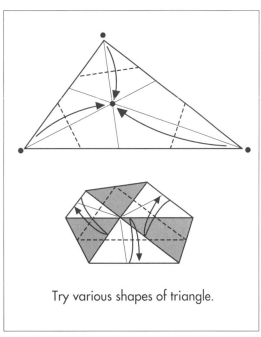

Try various shapes of triangle.

Drops

This unit looks like a raindrop. The basic folding method is the same as those of "Crosses" and "Trefoils."

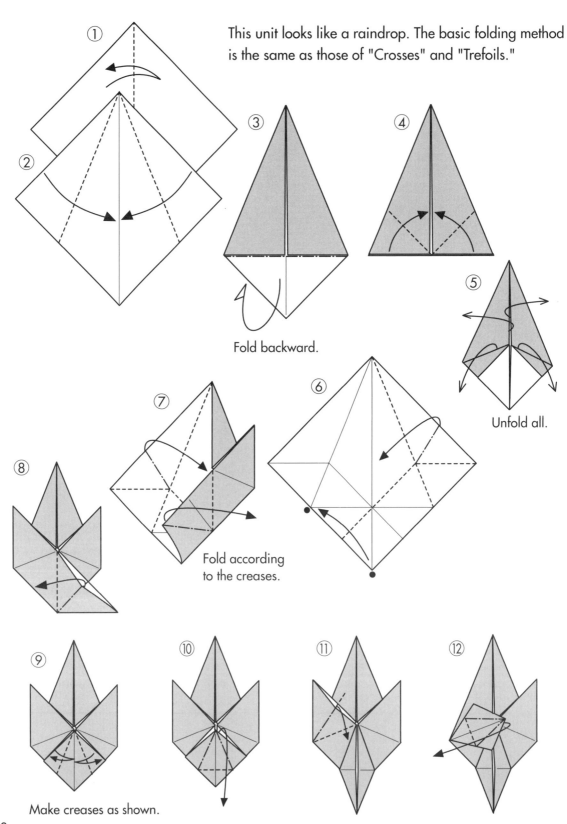

Fold backward.

Unfold all.

Fold according to the creases.

Make creases as shown.

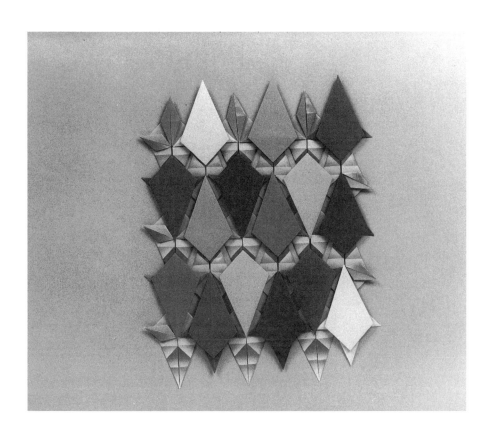

Fold the other flap
in the same way
as steps ⑪ and⑫.

⑬

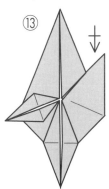

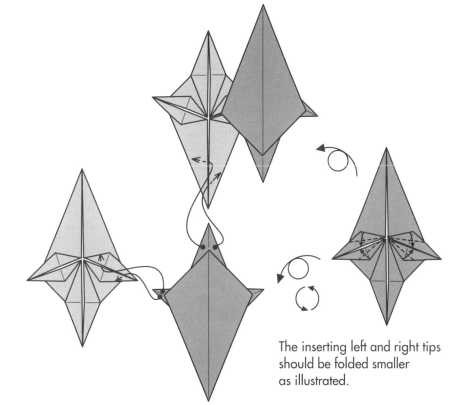

The inserting left and right tips
should be folded smaller
as illustrated.

49

► Variation of Drops ◄

True up the lengths of joining parts as illustrated.
Try various joining methods.

⑥ on page 16

[Cross] on page 16

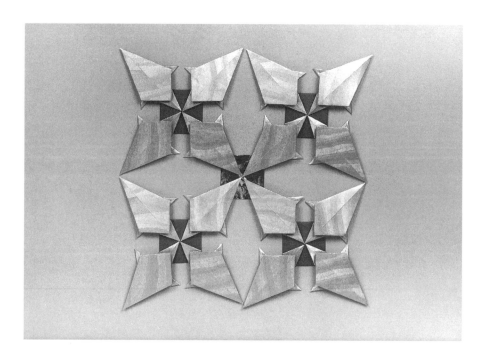

Blooming Flowers 1

Begin with step ⑨ on page 48.

It is a little troublesome to cut the paper,
but there is a singular fascination in this work.
The units extend inward and outward endlessly.

Unfold all after making creases.

▶ Jointing Unit 1 ◀

Insert into the slit.

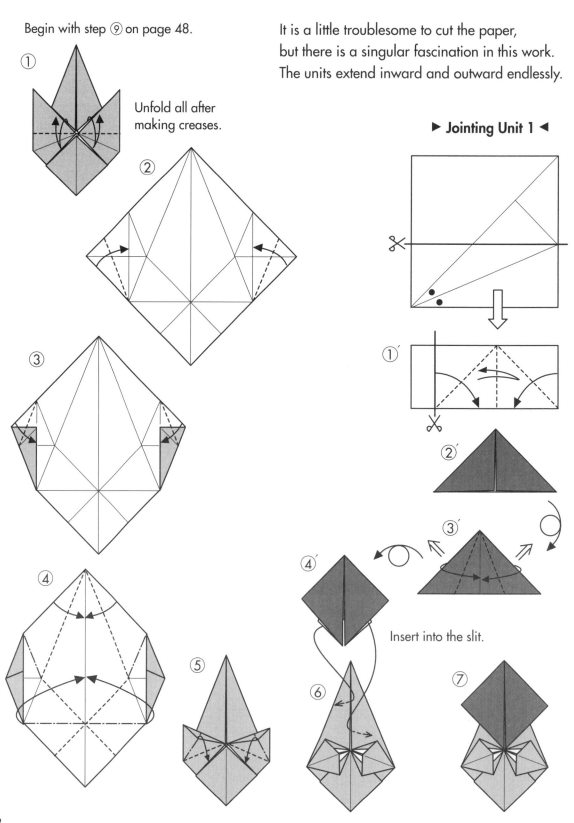

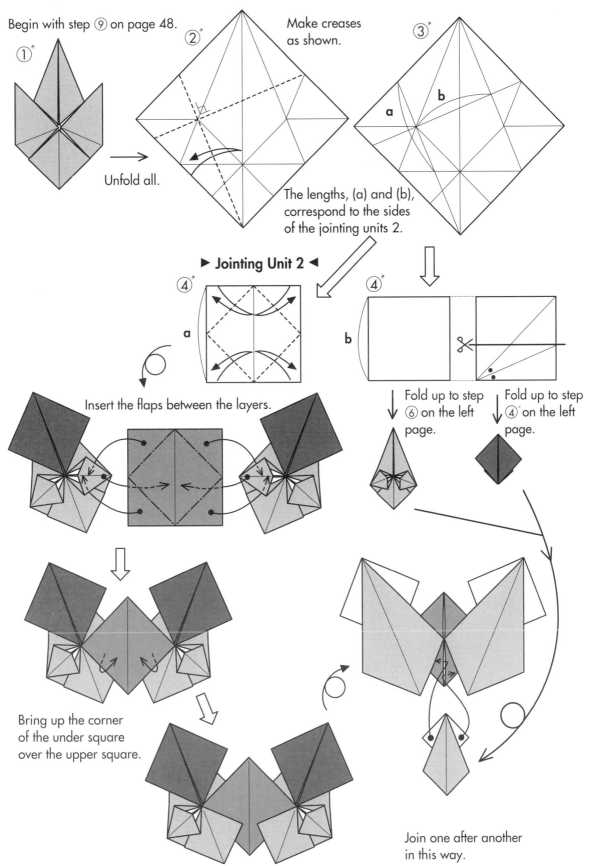

Begin with step ⑨ on page 48.

①˝

②˝ Make creases as shown.

Unfold all.

The lengths, (a) and (b), correspond to the sides of the jointing units 2.

③˝

a   b

▶ **Jointing Unit 2** ◀

④˝

a

④˝

b

✂

Fold up to step ⑥ on the left page.

Fold up to step ④˝ on the left page.

Insert the flaps between the layers.

Bring up the corner of the under square over the upper square.

Join one after another in this way.

53

Front

Back

Samples

54

Blooming Flowers 2

① Fold only one portion of the [Trefoil] on page 34 and unfold.

Fold only one portion of the "Trefoil" and then follow the instructions, cutting away extra corners. It is rather difficult to make this triangle.
Fold step ⑦ with exactness and make it a model for measuring other units.

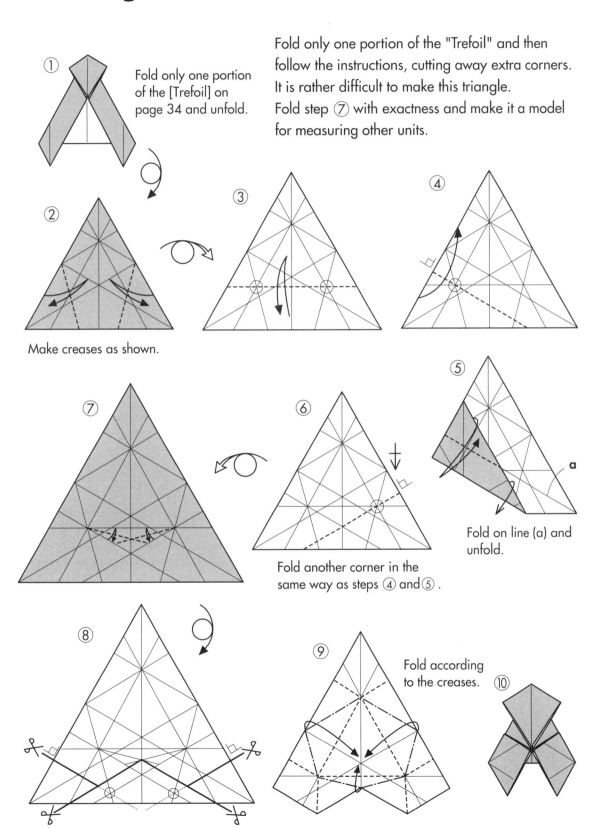

② Make creases as shown.

③

④

⑤ Fold on line (a) and unfold.

a

⑥ Fold another corner in the same way as steps ④ and ⑤.

⑦

⑧

⑨ Fold according to the creases.

⑩

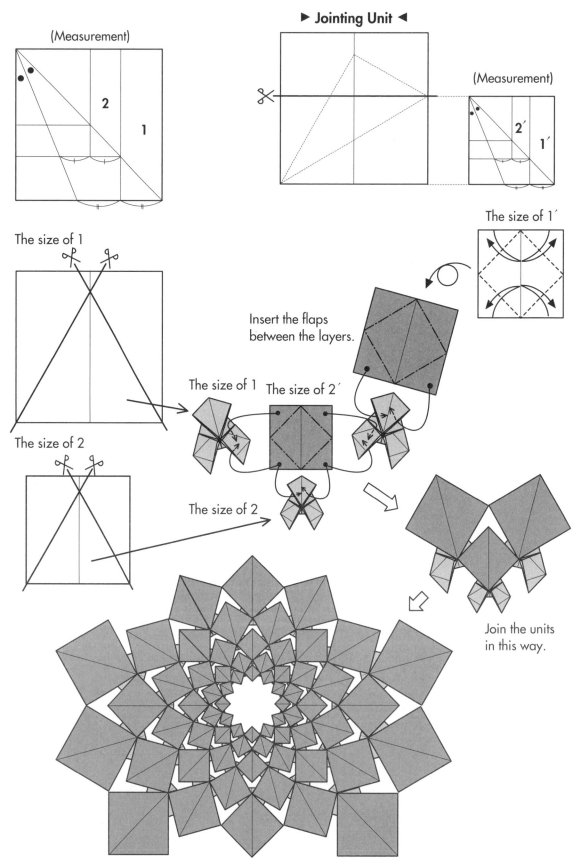

(Measurement)

► Jointing Unit ◄

(Measurement)

The size of 1´

The size of 1

The size of 2

The size of 1   The size of 2´

Insert the flaps
between the layers.

The size of 2

Join the units
in this way.

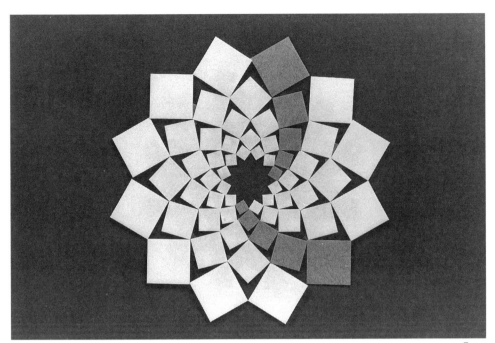

Front

Back

Pentagons with Slits

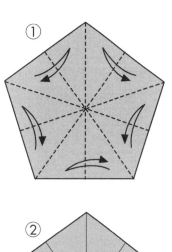

① ②

This is a pentagon unit. Bring out the horns by pulling out pleats of the folded pentagon as illustrated on the right page, and join with the "Pentagon with Slits."

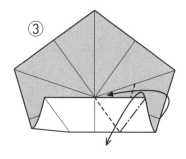

③

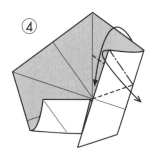

④

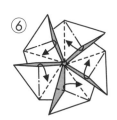

⑥

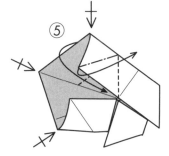

⑤

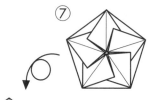

⑦

Unfold the whole.

Open and squash.

Fold the other three parts in the same way.

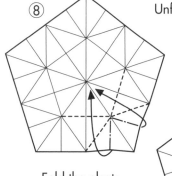

⑧

Fold the pleats inward.

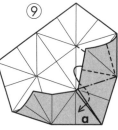

⑨

Tuck the folded pleat under (a).

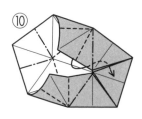

⑩

Continue folding in the same way.

[Pentagons with Slits

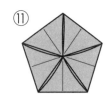

⑪

58

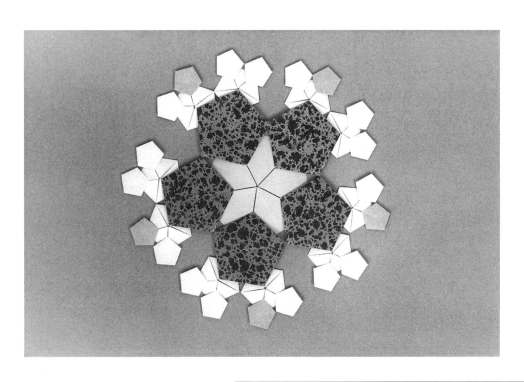

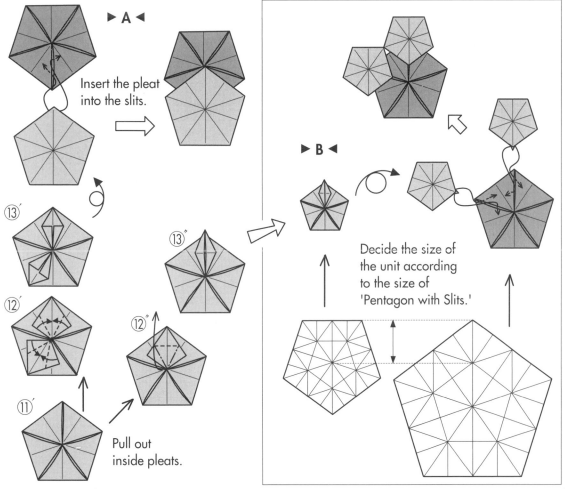

▶ A ◀

Insert the pleat into the slits.

⑬′

⑫′

⑪′

Pull out inside pleats.

⑫″

⑬″

▶ B ◀

Decide the size of the unit according to the size of 'Pentagon with Slits.'

Pentagons with Slits + Trefoils

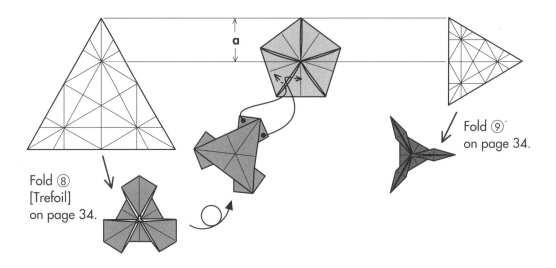

Fold ⑧
[Trefoil]
on page 34.

Fold ⑨´
on page 34.

The length of (a) corresponds to the portions of "Trefoils."
There are lots of variations. Enjoy the rhythmical designs.

Pentagons with Slits + Crosses

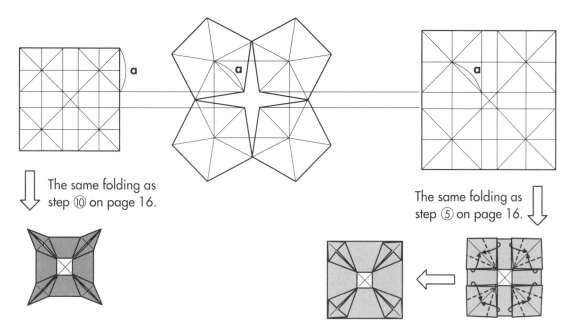

The same folding as step ⑩ on page 16.

The same folding as step ⑤ on page 16.

Let measurement (a) of the pentagon correspond to those of "Crosses."

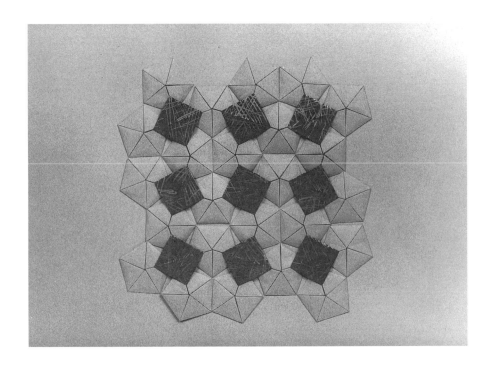

Pentagons with Slits joined on Top

There are various ways of joining this unit. It is a little fragile and that is a weak point of this unit.

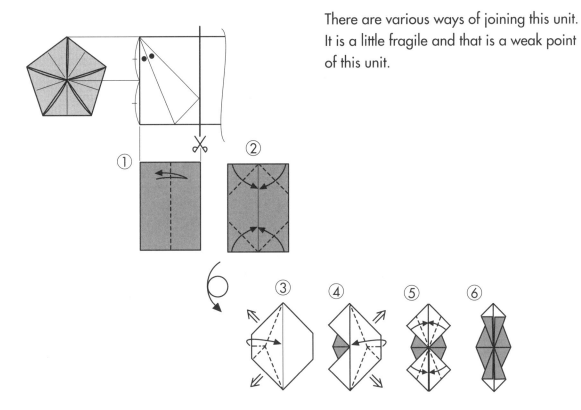

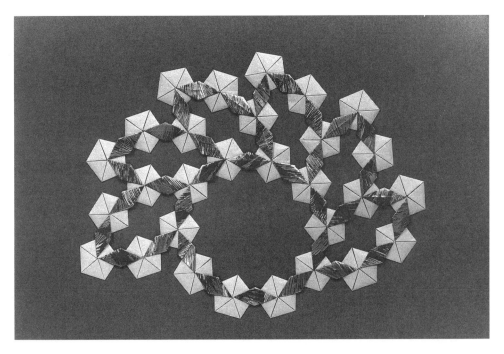

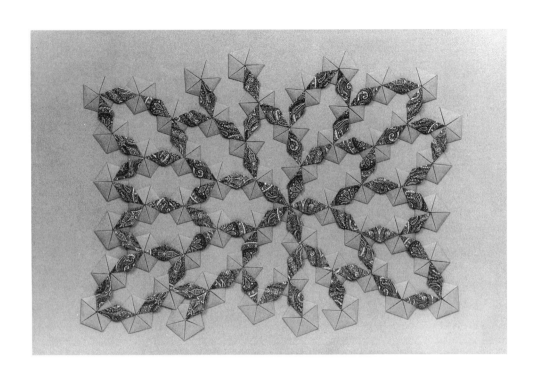

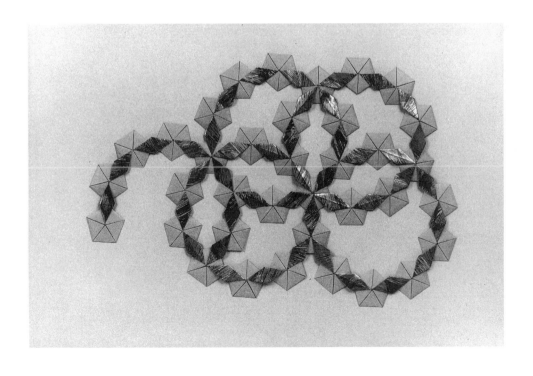

Pentagons with Slits joined on Side

There are various joining methods.
Introduced here is a sample worked out by Kodi Husimi.

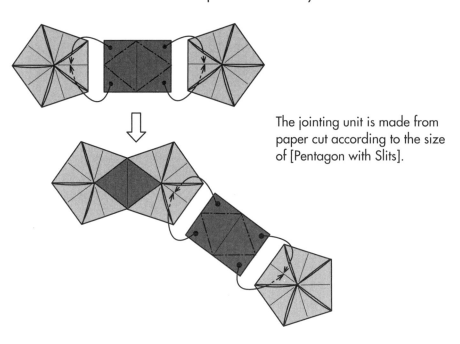

The jointing unit is made from paper cut according to the size of [Pentagon with Slits].

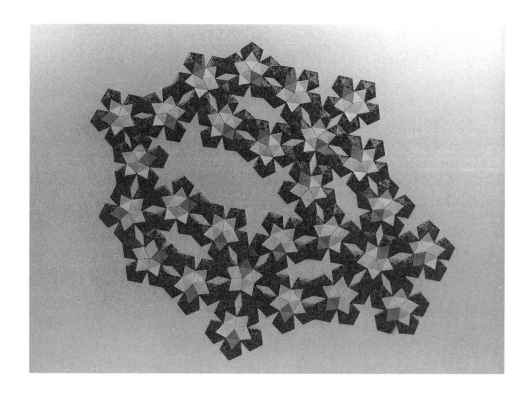

Windmills + Joints of 180°

This is one of my favorite works, since the units are locked firmly.
The result reveals an unexpected interesting shape, and there are wide variations.

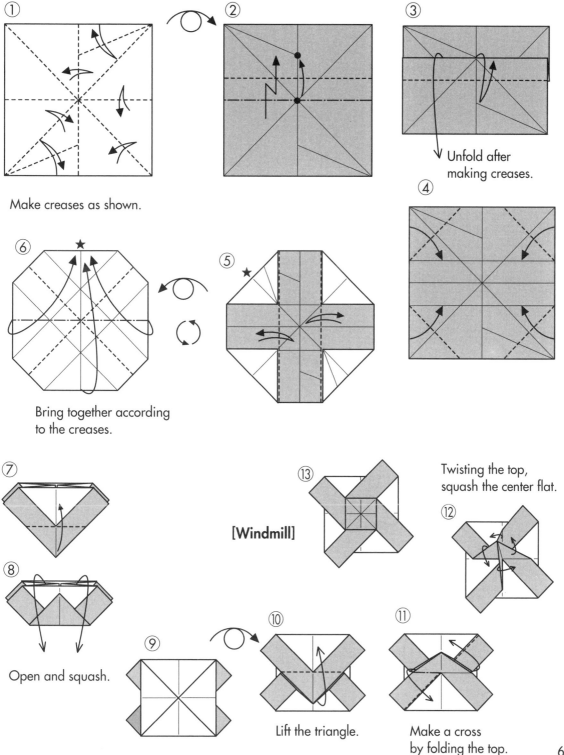

① Make creases as shown.

③ Unfold after making creases.

⑥ Bring together according to the creases.

⑧ Open and squash.

⑩ Lift the triangle.

⑪ Make a cross by folding the top.

Twisting the top, squash the center flat.

[Windmill]

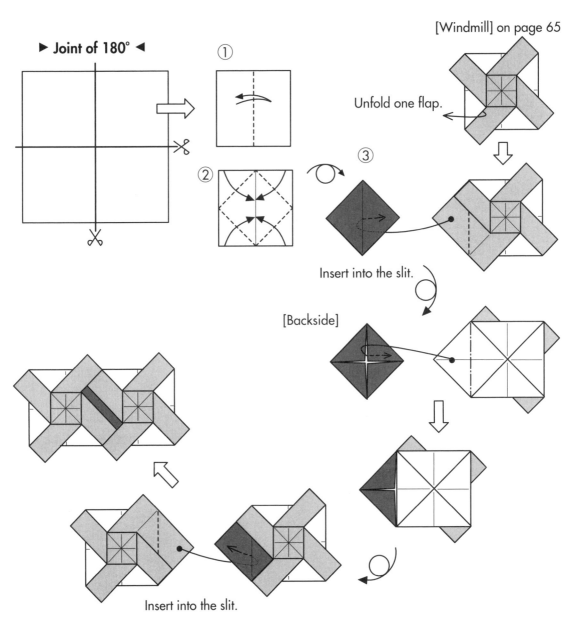

► **Joint of 180°** ◄

[Windmill] on page 65

Unfold one flap.

① ② ③

Insert into the slit.

[Backside]

Insert into the slit.

► **Variation of Windmill** ◄
< A >

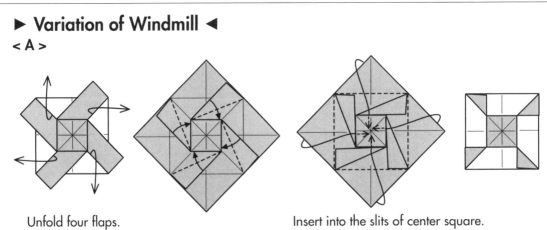

Unfold four flaps.

Insert into the slits of center square.

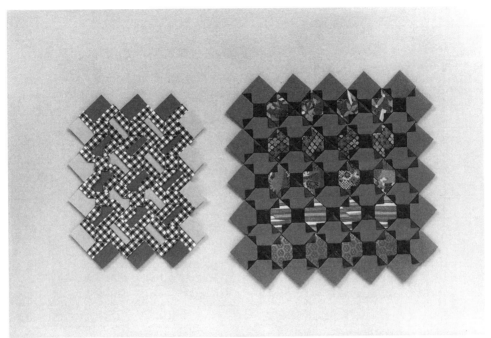

from left, Variations B, A

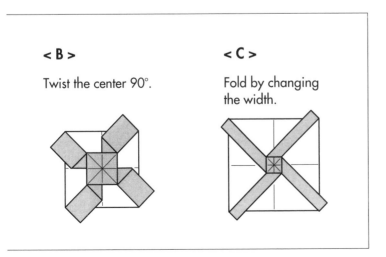

< B >

Twist the center 90°.

< C >

Fold by changing
the width.

Windmills + Joints of 135° and 120°

This unit can join octagons and hexagons.
The method is the same as that of "Windmill."
It is possible to mix with the joint of 180°.

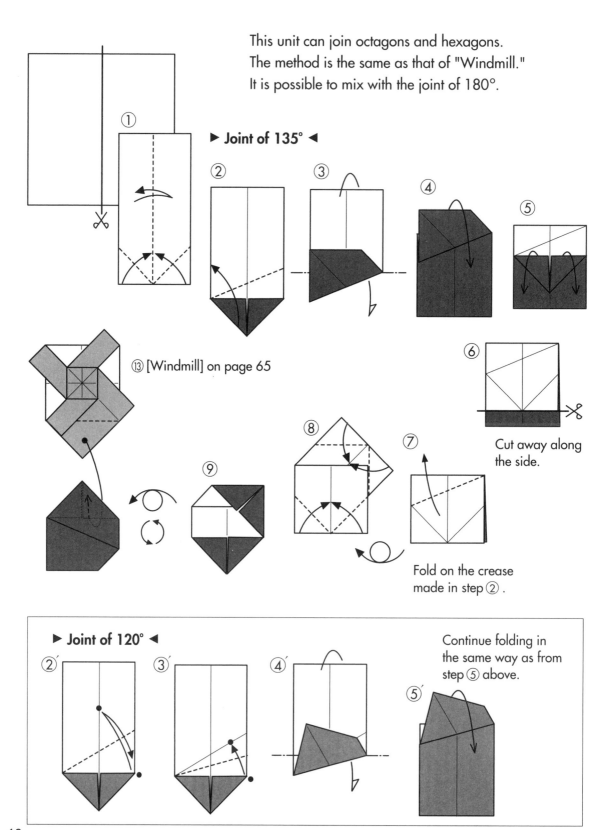

▶ Joint of 135° ◀

⑬ [Windmill] on page 65

⑥ Cut away along the side.

⑦ Fold on the crease made in step ②.

▶ Joint of 120° ◀

Continue folding in the same way as from step ⑤ above.

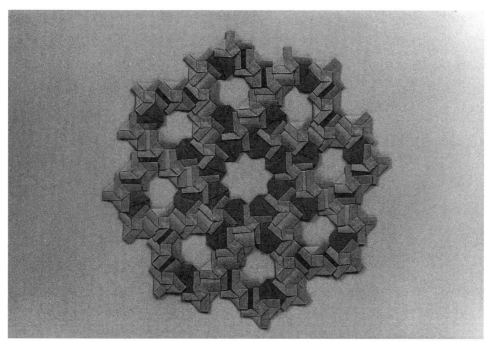

Joints of 135° and 180°

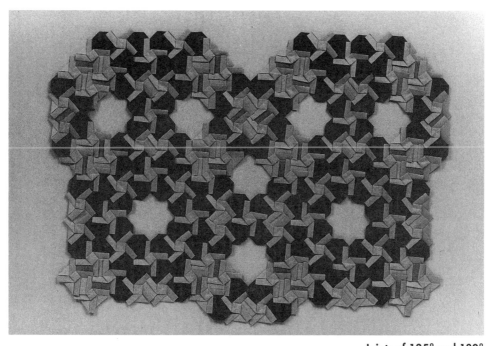

Joints of 135° and 180°

Star 1

Step ⑭ will make a good decoration. Fold, as you like. The view from back also looks interesting.

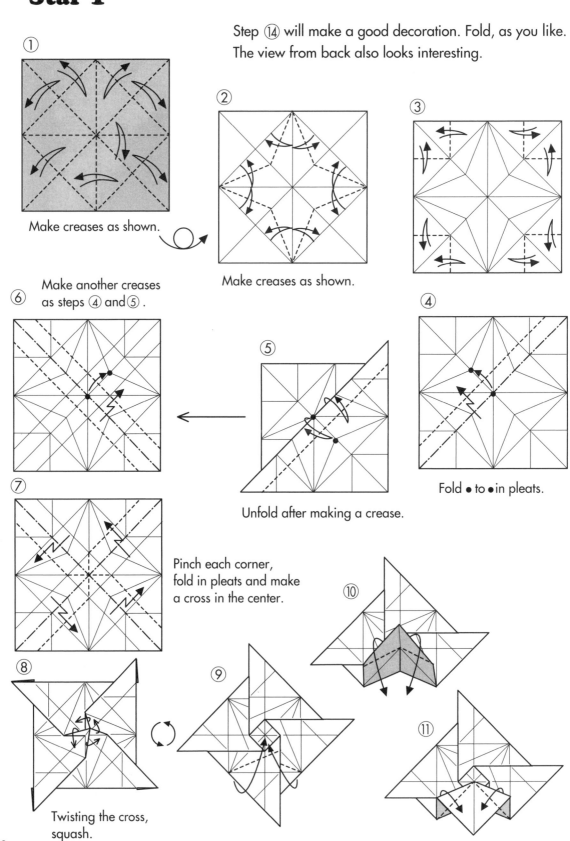

① Make creases as shown.

② Make creases as shown.

③

⑥ Make another creases as steps ④ and ⑤ .

⑤ Unfold after making a crease.

④ Fold ● to ● in pleats.

⑦ Pinch each corner, fold in pleats and make a cross in the center.

⑧ Twisting the cross, squash.

⑨

⑩

⑪

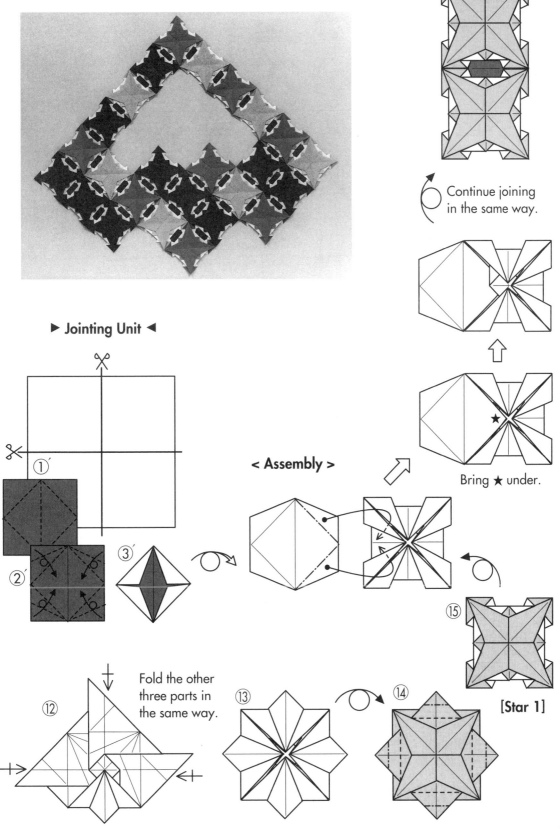

► **Jointing Unit** ◄

< Assembly >

Continue joining in the same way.

Bring ★ under.

Fold the other three parts in the same way.

[Star 1]

71

Star 2

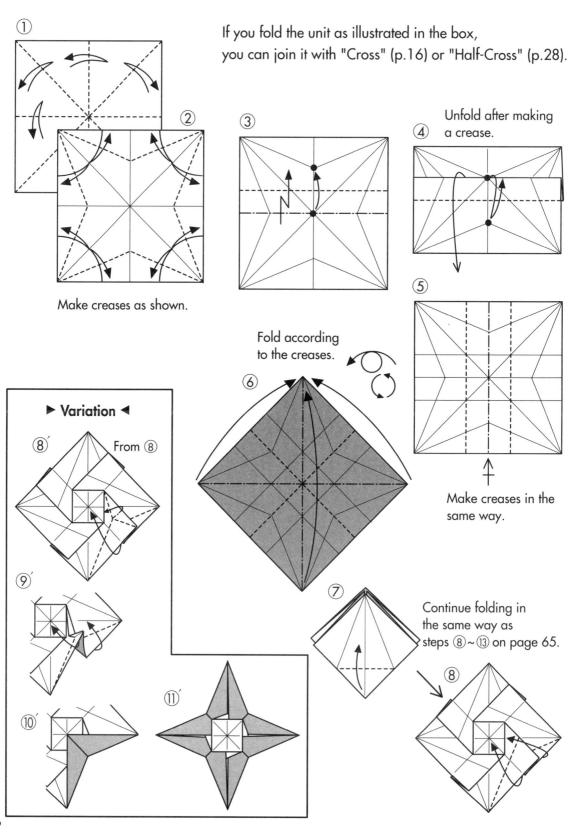

① Make creases as shown.

If you fold the unit as illustrated in the box,
you can join it with "Cross" (p.16) or "Half-Cross" (p.28).

②

③

④ Unfold after making a crease.

⑤ Make creases in the same way.

Fold according to the creases.

⑥

⑦ Continue folding in the same way as steps ⑧~⑬ on page 65.

⑧

▶ Variation ◀

⑧′ From ⑧

⑨′

⑩′

⑪′

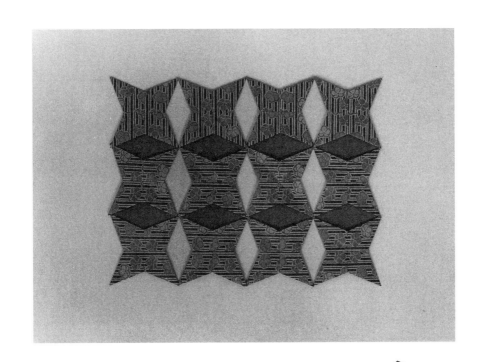

▶ **Jointing Unit** ◀

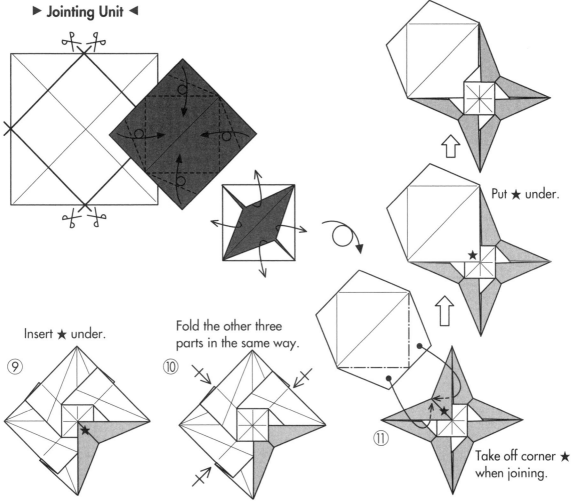

Put ★ under.

Insert ★ under.

⑨

Fold the other three
parts in the same way.

⑩

⑪

Take off corner ★
when joining.

Star 3

Begin with ⑪ on page 73.

Fold each tip of "Star 2" as illustrated and join.

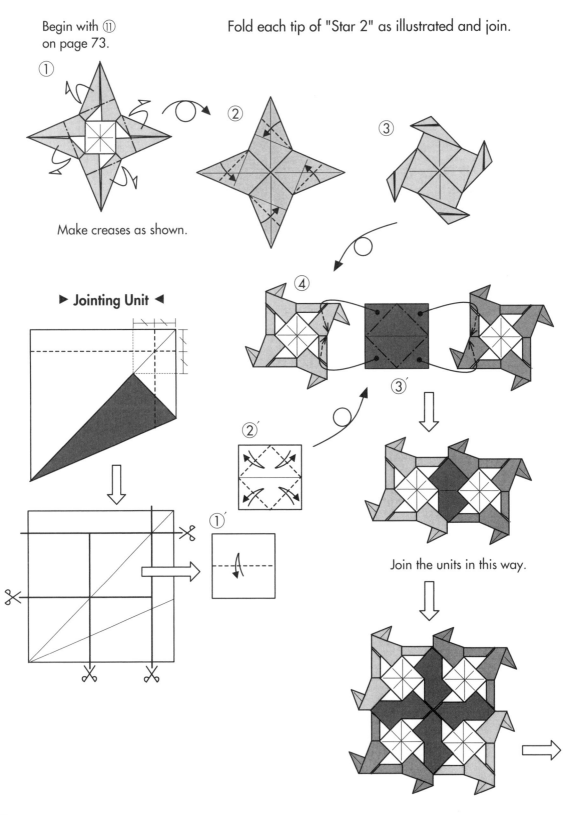

Make creases as shown.

▶ **Jointing Unit** ◀

Join the units in this way.

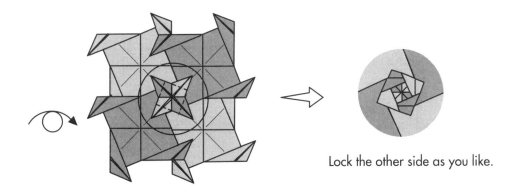

Lock the other side as you like.

Star 4

Make creases firmly as illustrated and proceed in order.
It will be a little difficult to make ⑨ from ⑧,
but try many times until you get the knack.

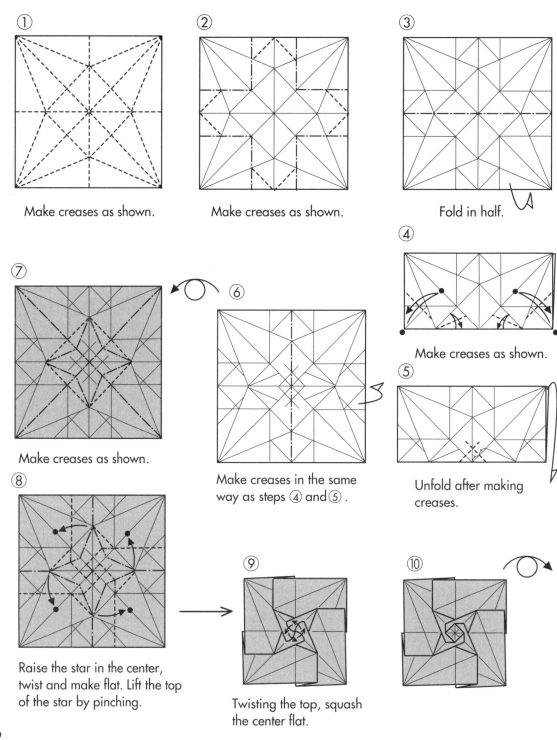

① Make creases as shown.

② Make creases as shown.

③ Fold in half.

④ Make creases as shown.

⑤ Unfold after making creases.

⑥ Make creases in the same way as steps ④ and ⑤.

⑦ Make creases as shown.

⑧ Raise the star in the center, twist and make flat. Lift the top of the star by pinching.

⑨ Twisting the top, squash the center flat.

⑩

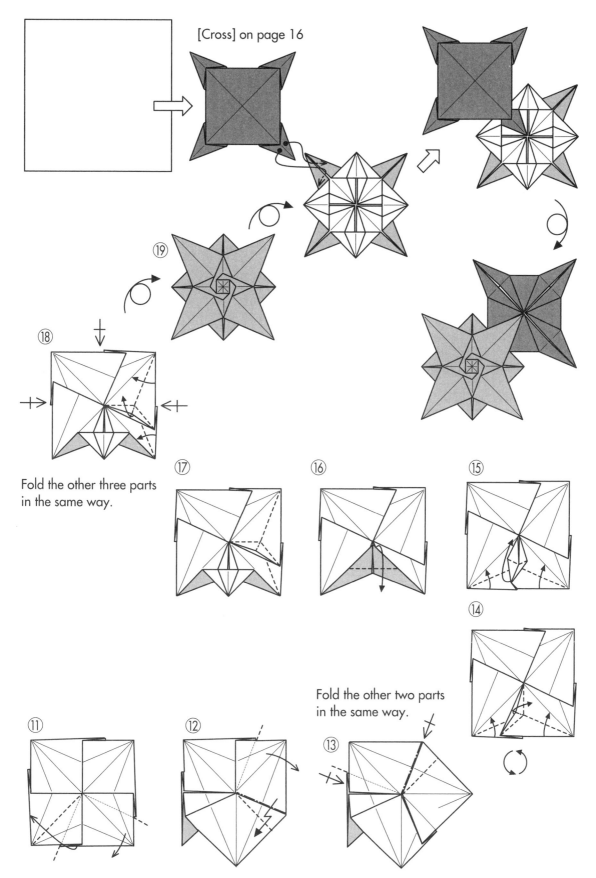

[Cross] on page 16

⑲

⑱

Fold the other three parts
in the same way.

⑰

⑯

⑮

⑭

Fold the other two parts
in the same way.

⑪

⑫

⑬

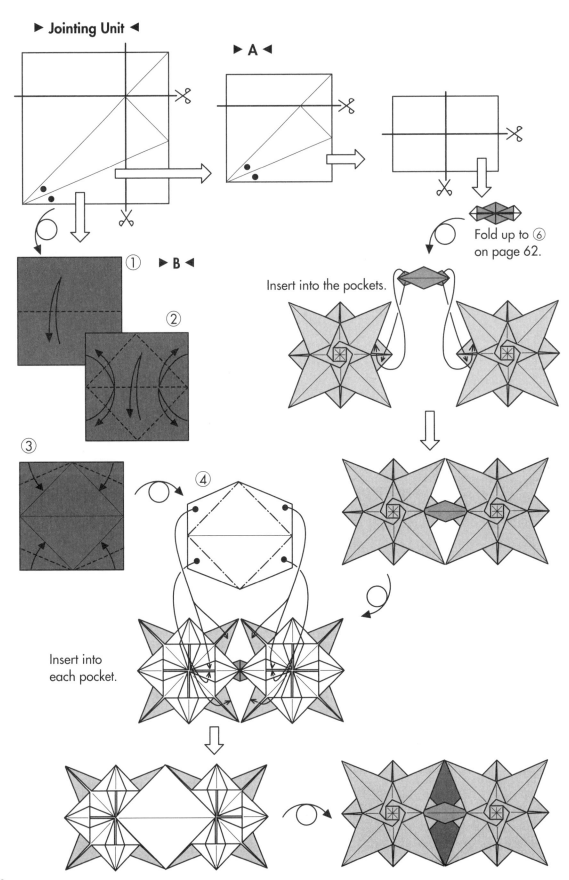

► Jointing Unit ◄

► A ◄

✂ Fold up to ⑥ on page 62.

Insert into the pockets.

① ► B ◄

②

③

④

Insert into each pocket.

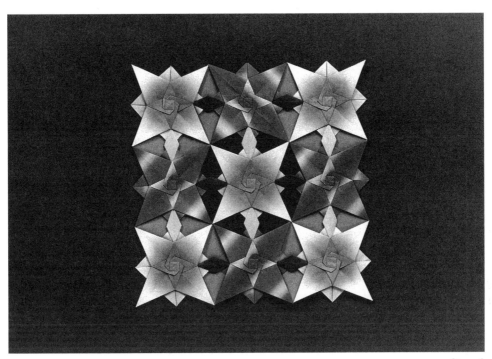

Stars 4

Stars 4 + Crosses

► Variation of Stars ◄

Just for reference, here are presented some samples of a little complicated star.

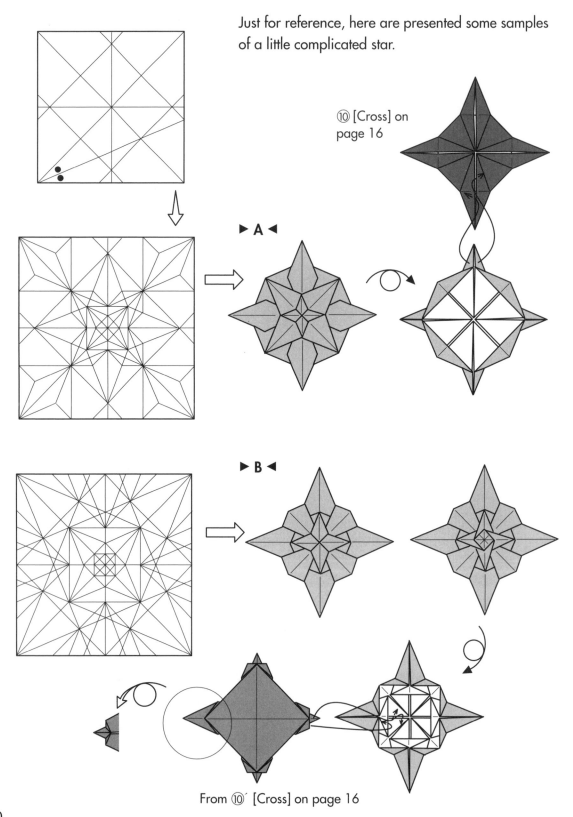

⑩ [Cross] on page 16

► A ◄

► B ◄

From ⑩´ [Cross] on page 16

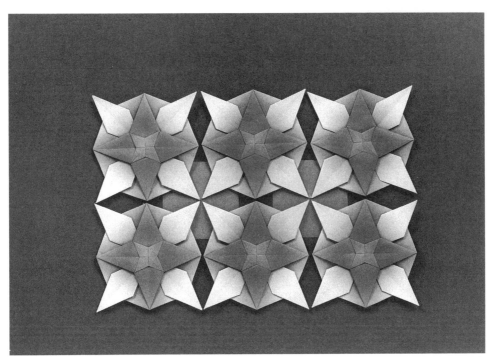

A

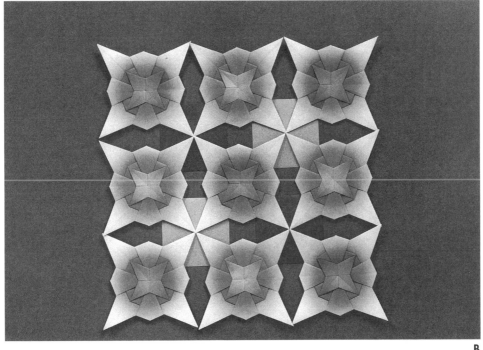

B

81

Hydrangea 1

Mr. Shuzo Fujimoto, a pioneer of 'twisting fold', and many others are working out methods of folding the center of paper, and some examples are introduced in the following series named 'hydrangea.' The application is interesting in terms of 'joining.'

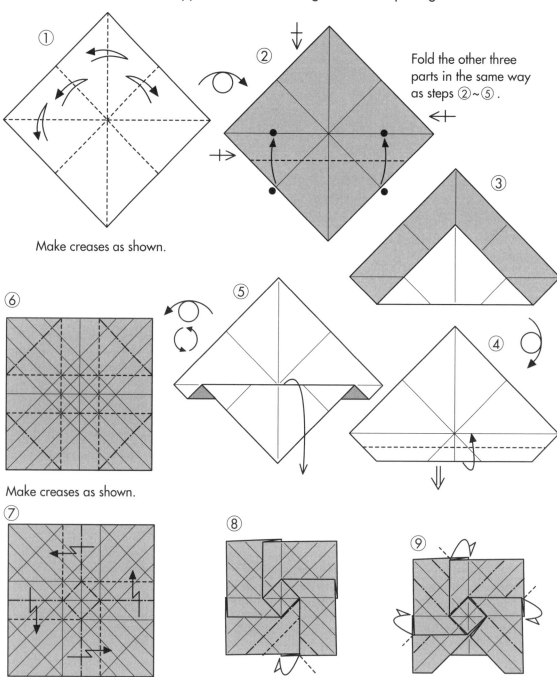

① Make creases as shown.

② Fold the other three parts in the same way as steps ②~⑤.

③

④

⑤

⑥ Make creases as shown.

⑦ Pinch center lines to make pleats and squash the center flat.

⑧ As if undoing, fold on creases and make pleats inward.

⑨ Fold the other three parts in the same way.

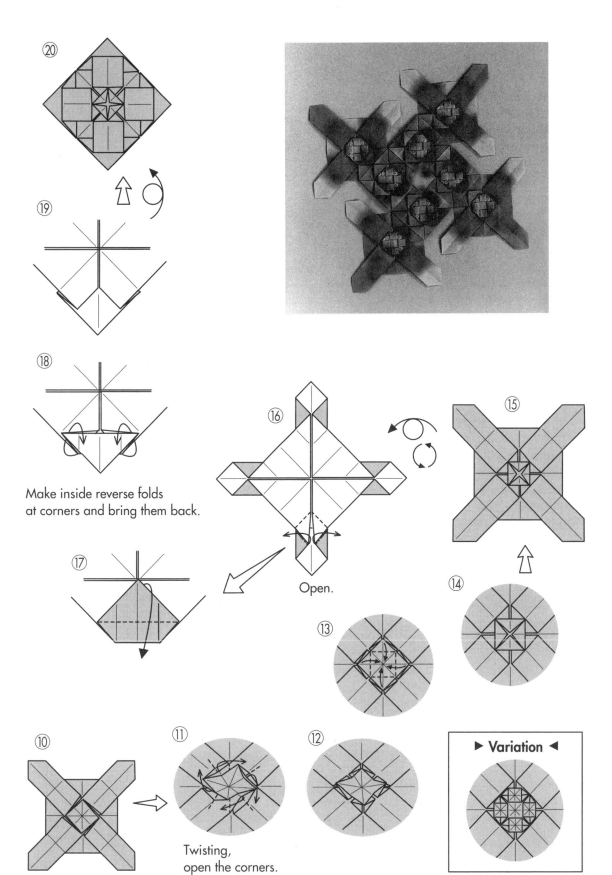

⑳

⑲

⑱

Make inside reverse folds
at corners and bring them back.

⑰

⑯

Open.

⑮

⑭

⑬

⑩

⑪

Twisting,
open the corners.

⑫

▶ **Variation** ◀

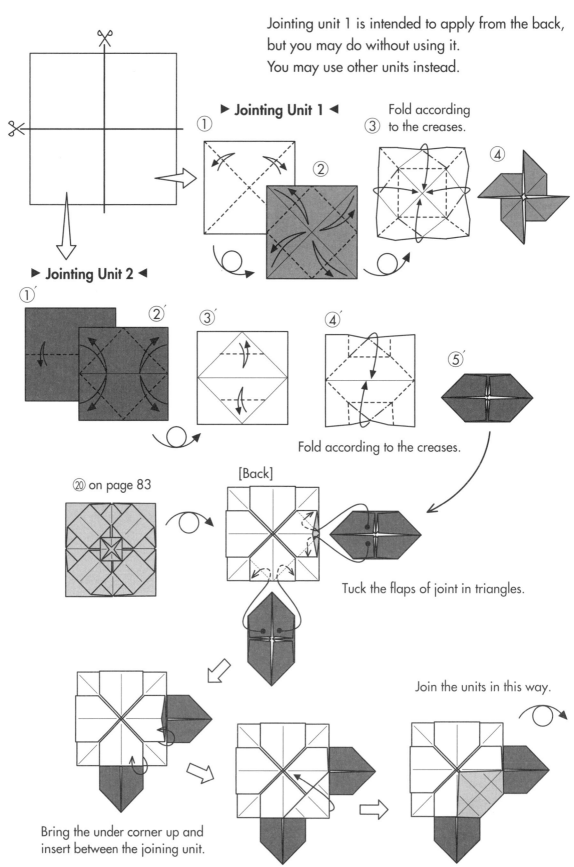

Jointing unit 1 is intended to apply from the back, but you may do without using it. You may use other units instead.

▶ **Jointing Unit 1** ◀

① ②

③ Fold according to the creases.

④

▶ **Jointing Unit 2** ◀

①´ ②´ ③´ ④´ ⑤´

Fold according to the creases.

⑳ on page 83

[Back]

Tuck the flaps of joint in triangles.

Bring the under corner up and insert between the joining unit.

Join the units in this way.

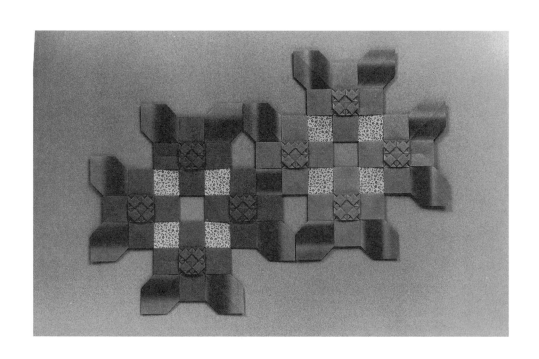

< How to join the back >

[Jointing Unit 1]

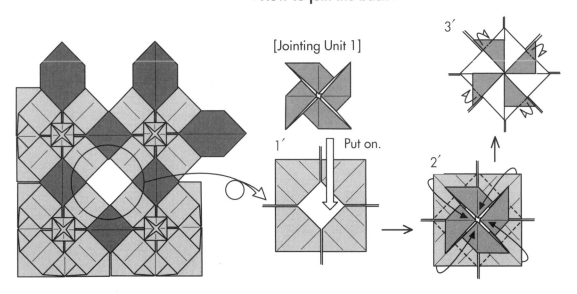

1´

Put on.

2´

3´

Hydrangea 2

Work out your own variations on the flower part in the center.
Jointing units are used as decorations.

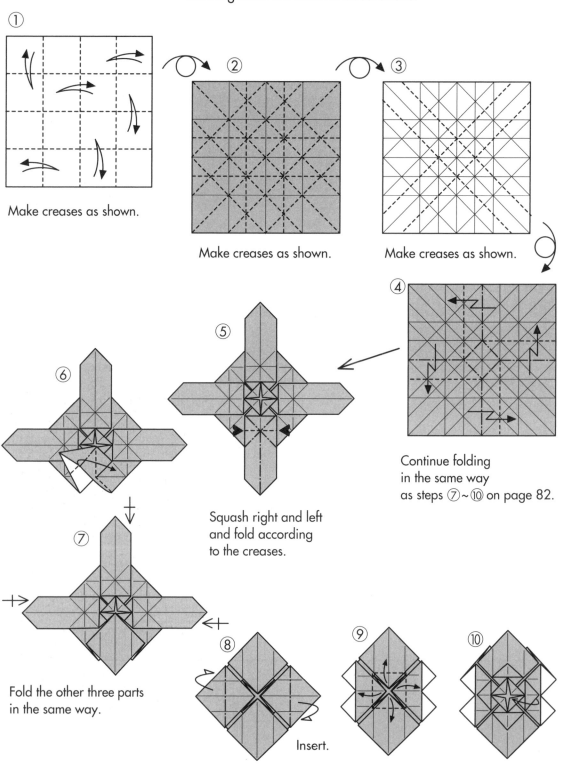

① Make creases as shown.

② Make creases as shown.

③ Make creases as shown.

④ Continue folding
in the same way
as steps ⑦~⑩ on page 82.

⑤ Squash right and left
and fold according
to the creases.

⑥

⑦ Fold the other three parts
in the same way.

⑧ Insert.

⑨

⑩

▶ Jointing Unit ◀

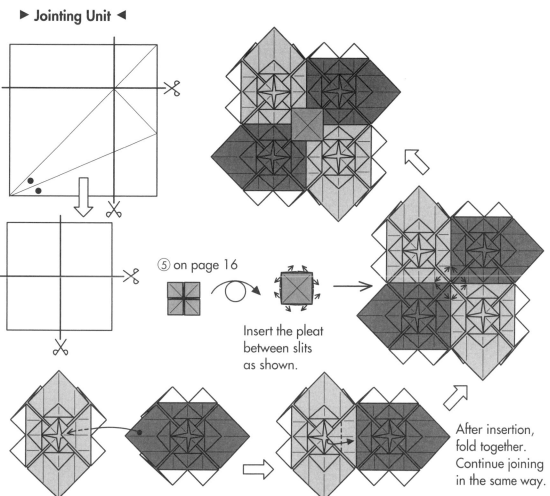

⑤ on page 16

Insert the pleat
between slits
as shown.

After insertion,
fold together.
Continue joining
in the same way.

ORIGAMI BOOKS
from Japan Publications

3D ORIGAMI: Step-by-step Illustrations by Yoshie Hatahira et al.
90 pp., 8 1/4 x 10 1/4 in., 24 pp. color, 64 pp. b/w photos and line drawings, paperback.
ISBN: 4-88996-057-0

BRILLIANT ORIGAMI: A Collection of Original Designs by David Brill
240 pp., 7 1/4 x 10 1/4 in., 8 pp. color, 215 pp. line drawings, paperback.
ISBN: 0-87040-896-8

COMPLETE ORIGAMI COLLECTION, THE, by Toshie Takahama
160 pp., 7 1/4 x 10 1/4 in., 8 pp. color, 147 pp. line drawings, paperback.
ISBN: 0-87040-960-3

CREATIVE ORIGAMI by Kunihiko Kasahara
180 pp., 8 1/4 x 11 3/4 in., 8 pp. b/w photos, 160 pp. line drawings, paperback.
ISBN: 0-87040-411-3

FABULOUS ORIGAMI BOXES by Tomoko Fuse
98 pp., 7 1/4 x 10 1/4 in., 8 pp. color, 80 pp. line drawings, paperback.
ISBN: 0-87040-978-6

HOME DECORATING WITH ORIGAMI by Tomoko Fuse
126 pp., 7 1/4 x 10 1/4 in., 16 pp. color, 104 pp. line drawings, paperback.
ISBN: 4-88996-059-7

JOYFUL ORIGAMI BOXES by Tomoko Fuse
96 pp., 7 1/4 x 10 1/4 in., 8 pp. color, 80 pp. line drawings, paperback.
ISBN: 0-87040-974-3

KUSUDAMA: Ball Origami by Makoto Yamaguchi
72 pp., 7 1/4 x 10 1/4 in., 8 pp. color, 65 pp. line drawings, paperback.
ISBN: 4-88996-049-X

MAGIC OF ORIGAMI, THE, by Alice Gray and Kunihiko Kasahara with cooperation of Lillian Oppenheimer and Origami Center of America
132 pp., 7 1/4 x 10 1/4 in., 122 pp. b/w photos and line drawings, paperback.
ISBN: 0-87040-624-8

ORIGAMI by Hideki Sakata
66 pp., 7 1/4 x 10 1/4 in., 66 pp. full color illustrations, paperback.
ISBN: 0-87040-580-2

ORIGAMI ANIMALS by Keiji Kitamura
88 pp., 8 1/4 x 10 1/4 in., 88 pp. full color illustrations, 12 sheets of origami paper included, paperback.
ISBN: 0-87040-941-7

ORIGAMI BOXES by Tomoko Fuse
72 pp., 7 1/4 x 10 1/4 in., 8 pp. color, 60 pp. line drawings, paperback.
ISBN: 0-87040-821-6

ORIGAMI CLASSROOM I by Dokuotei Nakano
Boxed set, board-book: 24 pp., 6 x 6 in., 24 pp. full color illustrations, plus origami paper: 6 x 6 in., 54 sheets of rainbow-color paper.
ISBN: 0-87040-912-3

ORIGAMI CLASSROOM II by Dokuotei Nakano
Boxed set, board-book: 24 pp., 6 x 6 in., 24 pp. full color illustrations, plus origami paper: 6 x 6 in., 60 sheets of rainbow-color paper.
ISBN: 0-87040-938-7

ORIGAMI FOR THE CONNOISSEUR by Kunihiko Kasahara and Toshie Takahama
168 pp., 7 1/4 x 10 1/4 in., 2 color line drawings, paperback.
ISBN: 4-8170-9002-2

ORIGAMI HEARTS by Francis Ow Mun Yin
120 pp., 7 1/4 x 10 1/4 in., 8 pp. color, 104 pp. line drawings, paperback.
ISBN: 0-87040-957-3

ORIGAMI MADE EASY by Kunihiko Kasahara
128 pp., 6 x 8 1/4 in., 113 pp. b/w photos and line drawings, paperback.
ISBN: 0-87040-253-6

ORIGAMI MAGIC TRICKS by Yoshihide Momotani (Pub. date: October 2001)
112 pp., 7 1/4 x 10 1/4 in., 16 pp. color, 89 pp. 2 color line drawings, paperback.
ISBN: 4-88996-078-3

ORIGAMI OMNIBUS: Paper-folding for Everybody by Kunihiko Kasahara
384 pp., 7 1/4 x 10 1/4 in., 8 pp. color, 360 pp. line drawings, paperback.
ISBN: 4-8170-9001-4

ORIGAMI TREASURE CHEST by Keiji Kitamura
80 pp., 8 1/4 x 10 1/4 in., full color, paperback.
ISBN: 0-87040-868-2

PAPER MAGIC: Pop-up Paper Craft by Masahiro Chatani
92 pp., 7 1/4 x 10 1/4 in., 16 pp. color, 72 pp. b/w photos and line drawings, paperback.
ISBN: 0-87040-757-0

PLAYFUL ORIGAMI by Reiko Asou
96 pp., 8 1/4 x 10 1/4 in., 48 pp. full color illustrations, 10 sheets of origami paper included, paperback.
ISBN: 0-87040-827-5

POP-UP GIFT CARDS by Masahiro Chatani
80 pp., 7 1/4 x 10 1/4 in., 16 pp. color, 64 pp. b/w photos and line drawings, paperback.
ISBN: 0-87040-768-6

POP-UP GEOMETRIC ORIGAMI by Masahiro Chatani and Keiko Nakazawa
86 pp., 7 1/4 x 10 1/4 in., 16 pp. color, 64 pp. b/w photos and line drawings, paperback.
ISBN: 0-87040-943-3

POP-UP ORIGAMIC ARCHITECTURE by Masahiro Chatani
88 pp., 7 1/4 x 10 1/4 in., 4 pp. color, 11 pp. b/w photos, 68 pp. line drawings, paperback.
ISBN: 0-87040-656-6

Quick & Easy ORIGAMI by Toshie Takahama
Boxed set, book: 60 pp.,, 6 x 6 in., 30 pp. color and 30 pp. line drawings, origami paper: 60 sheets in 6 colors.
ISBN: 4-88996-056-2

Quick & Easy ORIGAMI BOXES by Tomoko Fuse
Boxed set, book: 60 pp.,, 6 x 6 in., 30 pp. color and 30 pp. line drawings, origami paper: 60 sheets in 6 colors.
ISBN: 4-88996-052-X

UNIT ORIGAMI: Multidimensional Transformations by Tomoko Fuse
244 pp., 7 1/4 x 10 1/4 in., 8 pp. color, 220 pp. b/w photos and line drawings, paperback.
ISBN: 0-87040-852-6

WORLD OF ORIGAMI, THE, by Isao Honda
182 pp., 8 1/4 x 11 3/4 in., 170 pp. b/w photos and line drawings, paperback.
ISBN: 0-87040-383-4